PLAE SCORE™

Treasure Quest

SUSAN M. GOLTSMAN

SALLY MCINTYRE

DAVID DRISKELL

Illustrations by

DICK WILSON

MIG Communications
Berkeley, California

A Thematic Play and Learning Program for Children of All Abilities

MIG Communications, 1802 Fifth Street, Berkeley, CA 94710-1915, USA.
(510) 845-0953; fax (510) 845-8750

Managing Editor: David Driskell
Assistant Editor: Jacques Talbot
Cover and Page Design: Anne Endrusick; Tony Pierce
Instructional Illustrations: Tim Lehane
Production Assistant: Paul Yee; Stuart Easterling

Library of Congress Cataloging-in-Publication Data

Goltsman, Susan M.
    Treasure Quest PLAE score : a thematic play and learning program for
children of all abilities / Susan M. Goltsman, Sally McIntyre,
David Driskell ; illustrations by Dick Wilson.
      p.   cm.
   ISBN 0-944661-06-8 : $14.95
   1. Education, Elementary--Activity programs. 2. Curriculum
enrichment. 3. Treasure-trove--Case studies. 4. Active learning.
5. Play.   I. McIntyre, Sally. II. Driskell, David, 1963- .
III. PLAE, Inc. IV. Title.
LB1570.G646 1994
372.19--dc20   94-32791
                                               CIP

To The Reader: The authors, editors, publishers, contributors, and others involved in the preparation of this curriculum and document assume no risk or liability for incidents arising from the application of the information contained herein in any way whatsoever.

A

PLAE SCORE

is an

ORCHESTRATED SET

of

CHILDREN'S WORKSHOP

ACTIVITIES

based around

A THEME

CONTENTS

CONTENTS

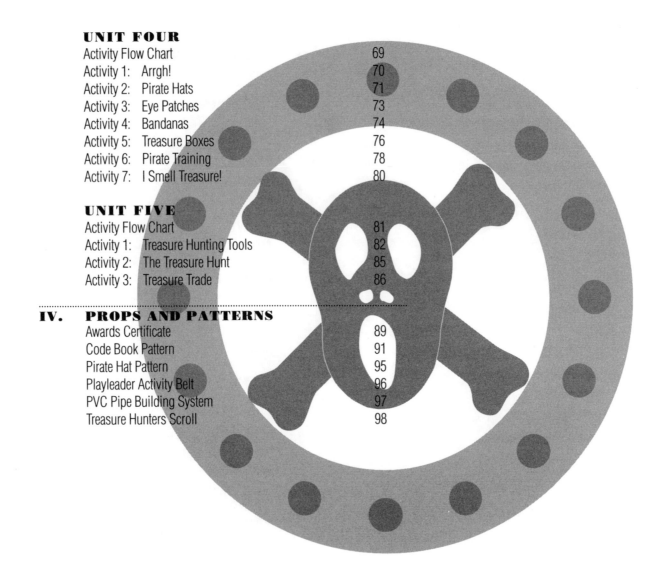

PLAE Score is a sequence of hands-on children's workshop activities based on a common theme. Developed in 1980 by Play and Learning in Adaptable Environments, Inc. (PLAE), PLAE Scores demonstrate how the physical environment, combined with a thematic program of activities, can facilitate human development and the integration of children with and without disabilities. The curriculum is designed for children ages five through twelve. However, the thematic model can easily be adapted for any age group, from preschool on up.

The PLAE Score Curriculum Guides were created to assist educators and recreation professionals in adapting the PLAE program model for their classrooms and recreation programs. The activities presented in each guide were developed by PLAE in its award-winning summer program in Berkeley, California. They have been field-tested by hundreds of professionals throughout the United States and Canada and thousands of children with and without disabilities.

Each PLAE Score is designed to achieve the following objectives:

- Facilitate the physical, social, emotional, and cognitive development of each child.

- Allow children to use, manipulate, and change their physical environment.

- Provide educational and recreational programs for children with special needs in the same physical and social setting that is appropriate and challenging for all children.

- Allow children to contribute their ideas and creativity to the curriculum.

- Incorporate multiple subject areas (language arts, science, math, physical education, theater, music, etc.) to provide program diversity and maximize learning opportunities.

- Engage children by allowing them to experience the fantasy theme.

- Structure activities to allow children of varying skill levels to succeed.

- Provide children with a choice of activities.

- Promote appreciation and understanding of human similarities and differences.

- Create an educational and recreational program that is fun!

PLAE Scores are organized in half-day units and presented over the course of a week. This overall structure, as well as the structure of each activity, can be adapted and altered for different group sizes, time requirements, facility constraints, educational goals, and special needs or interests. Even without alterations, children and staff will make spontaneous innovations once activities begin and they develop a sense of ownership and empowerment.

PLAE Scores are an exercise in creativity for both staff and children. We hope this PLAE Score provides a playful learning adventure you will want to return to again and again.

ACKNOWLEDGEMENTS

This PLAE Score was conceived and developed by the staff at PLAE, Inc.: Susan Goltsman, Executive Director; Sally McIntyre, Program Coordinator; and David Driskell, Communications Manager.

The authors would like to give a special round of applause to the playleaders who contributed to the development of this workshop concept: Gina Moreland, Barbara Walz, and Mimi Anderson.

Special recognition also goes to Frank Haeg, Director of Recreation for the City of Berkeley, his staff, and the Parks and Recreation Commission for the initial field-testing of the PLAE Scores.

Hats off to Robin Moore and Daniel Iacofano for their help in founding PLAE, Inc., with special thanks to Daniel for his work in developing the overall PLAE Score concept.

And finally, a standing ovation in honor of Barbara Lubin and Jackie Brand for demanding the right for their children to play.

I. Welcome to *Treasure Quest!*

AHOY, MATIES! COME ABOARD FOR THE ADVENTURE OF A LIFETIME!

Set sail for an exotic island in search of treasure!

TRIM THE JIB AND BATTEN THE HATCHES!

MEET THE GHOST OF LONG JOHN SILVER!

Solve the clues and discover untold riches!

In Treasure Quest, children create a fun-filled action adventure in which they are the heroes. Along the way, they build a ship and learn to be sailors. After arriving at their destination, they build shelters, become pirates, and create an island community. No matter what their ability or disability, they work together to solve the mystery of the buried treasure and share the bounty.

HIDDEN TREASURE!

ike any good story, a PLAE Score has a beginning, a middle, and an end. These program phases are called the orientation, the experience, and the culmination.

The Orientation (Unit One)

Orientation activities are designed to capture children's imaginations and create excitement about the pirate theme. Unit One begins with a large group meeting. Here the children sign aboard on the ship's log and listen to the story of Long John Silver and his vast treasure, hidden and forgotten on an island far away. Organized into a sailing crew, the children build a large treasure-hunting ship to take them to the island. Once the ship construction is underway, three PLAE Stations are set up. At the PLAE Stations, children can make telescopes, flags, and sails to help them on their journey. When everything is finished, the children gather in a large group once again for sailing songs. After singing several songs of the sea, they are interrupted by the appearance of the ghost of Long John Silver, who warns them that the treasure they seek is his and that they should turn back before disaster strikes.

The Experience (Units Two, Three, and Four)

The majority of *Treasure Quest* is dedicated to "the experience"—the sequence of activities in which children develop the treasure hunt theme by escaping the wreck of their ship, building an island community, and learning to be pirates. The experience is spread out over three program units.

- In Unit Two, the children find their ship sinking rapidly in a violent storm. To salvage their mission, they plan and build an escape course. They then work together to escape to the safety of a nearby island.

- In Unit Three, children are presented with the current situation on the island. Because there is no system of support on the island, they must build shelters and develop an island community that will help them survive and successfully face the island's roving bands of pirates. After building their shelters and developing their community's identity, the children make peanut butter balls and share ghost stories. The islanders then celebrate their new community with the first ever Island Highland Games, concluding with a grand awards ceremony in which everyone is a winner.

- In Unit Four, the children gather for a large group meeting where they are met by an old friend of Long John Silver. He warns them that unless they become pirates themselves, they will be overtaken by other pirates and never find the buried treasure. The children prepare to become pirates as they make pirate hats, eye patches, bandanas, and treasure boxes. Then they're ready for pirate training. The unit ends with another large group meeting, in which the children are briefed on the upcoming treasure hunt.

The Culmination (Unit Five)

The culmination activities provide the program's peak experience and a sense of closure. In *Treasure Quest,* the program culminates with the actual treasure hunt. Children receive their treasure hunting gear—a compass, a site map, and a code book—and their first clues. After much deciphering, decoding, thinking, and exploring, the treasure hunters find the buried treasure. They open the chests, divide and trade their bounty, and head for home, richer and wiser.

Unit Structure

Like the overall program structure, each unit has a beginning, a middle, and an end. The activities that comprise each unit are classified as orientation activities, experience activities, and culmination activities.

Orientation Activity

Each unit begins with an orientation activity. During this activity the stage is set for the thematic adventure and children are introduced to the unit's events. If a single unit is conducted over the course of several days, each day should begin with an orientation activity. The orientation activities in Unit One include signing up as a crewmember and hearing the story of Long John Silver and his long-lost treasure.

Experience Activity

This is an activity that develops the workshop's thematic experience. Different experience activities are often conducted simultaneously in the form of PLAE Stations. PLAE Stations are self-contained activity stations that allow children to move freely or on a rotating basis from activity to activity. They also help break up large groups into smaller working groups. In Unit One, children experience the beginning of their treasure hunt by building a ship; making telescopes, flags, and sails; and singing songs of the sea.

Culmination Activity

A culmination activity provides a peak experience and provides a sense of closure. The culmination activity for Unit One is the "Shipwreck," in which the ghost of Long John Silver makes an appearance and warns of impending doom.

Figure 1 provides an overview of *Treasure Quest,* illustrating the orientation/experience/culmination structure of both the program as a whole and each individual unit.

In every unit, children produce something tangible or learn a skill that can be shared with others. These created objects and new skills are considered the "products" of that unit and are an important element of the program's structure. Products give children a sense of accomplishment and help increase parent awareness of the program. This, in turn, can help extend the program's educational benefits by encouraging parents to participate in related activities with their children at home.

	UNIT ONE *Orientation*	TIME	UNIT TWO *The Experience*	TIME	UNIT THREE *The Experience*	TIME	UNIT FOUR *The Experience*	TIME	UNIT FIVE *Culmination*	TIME
ORIENTATION An activity which introduces the day or week	Treasure Quest!	20 min	We've Gotta Get Outta Here!	15 min	An Island Community	10 min	Arrgh!	15 min	Treasure Hunting Tools	30 min
THE EXPERIENCE Cumulative or chronological activities which develop the theme	Shipbuilding Telescopes Flags Billowing Sails Sailing Songs	120 min 15 min	The Escape Course	90 min	Village Building Village Identity Island Eats Ghost Stories Island Highland Games	45 min 20 min 30 min 45 min	Pirate Hats Eye Patches Bandanas Treasure Boxes Pirate Training	90 min 45 min	The Treasure Hunt	90 min
CULMINATION ACTIVITY Activity which creates a sense of closure, results in a final product or produces a peak experience	Shipwreck! Clean-up	10 min 15 min	The Escape Clean-up	60 min 15 min	Awards Ceremony Clean-up	15 min 15 min	I Smell Treasure! Clean-up	15 min 15 min	Treasure Trade Clean-up	30 min 30 min
THE PRODUCT Item child creates to take home or share with others					Award				Treasure	

Figure 1: Overview of the Treasure Quest PLAE Score

With creative playleadership, all children—with and without disabilities—can participate in PLAE Score activities. Playleaders should have high expectations for every child and encourage all children to perform each activity as independently as possible. By relating to children with disabilities with sensitivity and respect, playleaders can serve as role models for nondisabled children.

Every child is different. Abilities and disabilities are unique. Therefore, methods for effectively involving each child in the play experience must take individual needs into account. Before beginning each unit, identify activity requirements which may need to be modified for individual participants. Activity analysis is a technique commonly used by recreation professionals who adapt activities for individuals with special needs. Always assume that there is a way to involve everyone. Although some children may require one-to-one assistance, a playleader should never just complete an activity for a child. In certain extreme cases, when children's disabilities prevent them from doing part of an activity themselves, they should direct the person who is assisting them.

When in doubt about how to adapt an activity for a particular child, ask the child or the parent how similar activities have been adapted in the past. You might also consult a guidebook. An excellent guidebook for activity analysis is *Therapeutic Recreation Program Design Principles and Procedures* by Scout Gunn and Carol Ann Peterson (Englewood, NJ: Prentice Hall, 1978). If additional assistance is needed, contact your organization's recreation therapist or special education staff. If your agency does not have a qualified resource person, contact PLAE, Inc., your state professional organization for park and recreation professionals, or a local nonprofit organization which offers programs for individuals with disabilities for assistance.

Following are some critical considerations that will help you ensure that all children are involved to the greatest extent possible in your program's activities.

Facility Access

The facility in which the program is operated must be accessible to all children. All activity areas must be evaluated for accessibility and modifications made where necessary. The entire range of physical elements (e.g., ground surfaces, tables, stage areas, sinks, etc.) must be considered. In particular, an accessible restroom must always be provided. *The Accessibility Checklist* by Susan Goltsman, Tim Gilbert, and Steve Wohlford (Berkeley, CA: MIG Communications, 1993) is one tool which can be used to evaluate your facility for compliance with accessibility guidelines, including the requirements of the Americans with Disabilities Act (ADA).

Accessibility must be considered in conjunction with child development goals and benefits. For example, children who use wheelchairs or have difficulty walking require a firm, level surface for maximum mobility. This does not mean, however, that activities can never take place on grass, dirt, or other, more challenging surfaces. All children benefit from contact with varying textures and materials. Many children with disabilities can maneuver on grass or dirt surfaces either by themselves or with minimal assistance. The important thing is to consider the abilities and needs of each child and to avoid placing artificial limitations on his or her abilities and experiences. However, be sure to provide an accessible ground surface whenever a high level of mobility is required or public attendance is anticipated.

Be aware of children's needs and be prepared to respond accordingly. It is important to approach children with respect and sensitivity. When it appears that a child needs assistance on a challenging surface, be sure to ask permission before pushing the child's wheelchair. You should also have extra wheelchairs, benches, or folding chairs available so that children with disabilities can rest when necessary. Chairs at PLAE Stations are a particularly good way to integrate children with and without disabilities; having everyone on the same level encourages communication.

A high level of integration can be ensured simply by planning ahead and organizing your facility and activities appropriately. Be sure that the structure of activities and the organization of the facility and equipment allow children with disabilities to work side by side with other children. Social integration cannot occur if physical integration is not provided.

Equipment

Every activity has its own equipment requirements. In many cases, children with disabilities can use the same equipment as other participants. Frequently, children who need special equipment may already have this equipment for use at school or home. If not, simple adaptations can often be made. Examples of adaptations include using foam or "squishy" balls instead of hard rubber balls, increasing the width of a pencil or paintbrush for easy gripping, lowering targets for throwing, and enlarging print materials on a photocopy machine for children with limited vision. When adapted

equipment is used frequently by your organization, it should be stored in a central location accessible to all program staff.

Physical Skills

Evaluate activities to identify the physical skills required and make adaptations as necessary.

Strategies for integrating children with visual disabilities include providing verbal rather than visual cues and helping children learn to rely on other senses as they explore the environment or participate in the activity. Playleaders can provide one-on-one assistance as needed, such as offering an arm to escort a child to the next activity.

Children with mobility limitations can be integrated in a number of ways. If a tag game is planned and some children use wheelchairs or other walking aids, fast walking can be substituted for running as a way of integrating those children into the game. Some children may be able to get out of their wheelchairs for some activities (some may need assistance in transferring). Encourage children to position themselves in a way that makes them most comfortable and brings them as close as possible to other children.

When a child is not using her wheelchair or other disability equipment, make sure that other children do not play with it. Teach children that using personal belongings without permission is never good manners. Disability equipment is very expensive to replace and the child with a disability depends on it. Serious accidents occur from unsupervised use. Playing a supervised game, such as wheelchair relays with wheelchairs belonging to the agency, can be used as a disability awareness strategy.

Cognitive Skills

Activities vary in the degree of complex reasoning required for success. Success in some activities is based on luck or participation, such as playing Old Maid or simple board games, doing an abstract art project, or playing a simple cooperative game. Other activities require skills such as reading, analyzing, comparing, or predicting. For children with cognitive disabilities, activities or instructions may need to be simplified. The process used is similar to adapting activities for younger children. For example, instead of asking an open-ended question when involving children in planning activities, provide cues by including several possible answers in your question. If you are planning an escape from a shipwreck with the children, you might ask "Are there sharks in the water or is there an underwater cave?"

Do not separate children with cognitive limitations from other children in their age group. Encourage them to participate in age-appropriate activities that challenge them without overburdening them. There are a number of things you can do to help children with cognitive limitations participate in age-appropriate activities. One strategy is to incorporate the use of several senses—touch, sound, smell, taste—to help clarify an activity. Another strategy is to help children explore the activity individually before participating with the group. This helps reduce fears that result from encountering the unknown. Regardless of the strategy employed, children with cognitive disabilities need to be encouraged and supported. They also need to be closely supervised (without detracting from the play experience), since they can easily be victimized by other children.

Communication Skills

Communication is an important part of PLAE Score programs and is essential for integrating children with and without disabilities. If a child has difficulty communicating, find out from the child, his parents, or professionals what methods he uses for communication, and learn how you can interact with him. Common methods include sign language, pointing to pictures or letters on communication boards, and talking computers. Encourage the child to communicate in the group, and encourage other children to communicate with him on a one-to-one basis.

If a child is deaf or hearing-impaired and uses sign language, an interpreter should be available to interpret activity directions and conversation. Teach other children how to communicate with the deaf child through an interpreter. The program itself can become a vehicle for teaching children how to communicate directly with deaf children and adults. For example, children can be taught the signs for activities, materials, and program events.

Social Skills

As children grow and develop, they progress from playing alone to playing in pairs to playing in large groups. Through development and opportunities for interaction, most children gain the social and cooperative skills necessary to participate in small and large groups. However, some children may have difficulty with group participation. Adapt large group activities by providing children with options to participate in pairs or small groups when needed. Work on participation in large group activities as a long term goal.

Emotional Controls

Some children have difficulty managing their emotions. Emotional responses to activities are difficult to predict. Request that parents alert staff to situations which may be difficult for their child. Analyze activities for situations which may cause anger (e.g., physical contact, losing), fear (e.g., no option for not completing an activity without losing face), or frustration (e.g., waiting for a turn, activities that are too difficult). Situations which may cause negative emotions can thus be minimized, or eliminated when necessary.

Reducing situations which cause negative emotions in some children can create a more positive emotional environment for all children. For example, if the playleader divides children into teams, no one will be chosen last by a peer. A cooperative game can be substituted for a highly competitive game. When fear is involved, always provide less stressful options, such as performing in a group instead of alone.

Often, children actively test limits during the initial days of a workshop. Keep children firmly grounded in reality and make limits firm and consistent. All children should learn to resolve conflicts through verbalization. Playleaders should provide assistance in conflict resolution whenever necessary.

Some children may disrupt activities by talking or just making distracting comments. Encourage children to listen to what others are saying. Giving the disruptive child a job, such as holding the markers for the recorder, stabilizing the facilitation board, or illustrating other children's comments on the facilitation board, provides a positive means for the child to receive attention. It is important to keep children with short attention spans involved in the group activity as much as possible.

Competition and challenge are part of life and should not be eliminated; but each child should be allowed to set her own challenges and strive to achieve them. Children who have difficulty controlling their emotions need controlled challenges.

Treasure Quest provides a fantasy setting that can incorporate activities from many curriculum subjects. It is an ideal vehicle for whole-language activities and child-directed curricula. It also provides opportunities to introduce interdisciplinary concepts such as cultural awareness, career awareness, communication skills, environmental awareness, problem-solving skills, and the development of social skills and values. Above all, Treasure Quest and other PLAE Scores provide an active, hands-on approach that makes learning fun.

In Treasure Quest, the basic curriculum framework incorporates drama and theater arts, physical education, visual arts, and problem solving. This framework can easily be extended to include language arts, science, mathematics, history, and other subjects. The specific educational benefits of Treasure Quest and ways to extend the activities to include other subjects are discussed below.

Problem Solving

Treasure Quest provides numerous opportunities for incorporating a wide range of curriculum subjects in exciting and fun problem solving exercises. Children work together to build a ship, escape to safety, create a community, and find the treasure. In the process, children investigate the environment, learn to work together as a team, answer riddles, and piece together various clues (see "Mathematics" on the following page). Ultimately, they solve the mystery and find the treasure.

Drama and Theater Arts

Drama and theater arts are emphasized throughout Treasure Quest. By participating in thematically linked activities throughout the workshop, children learn to observe, experience, and respond to dramatic elements, actions, and characterizations. By developing costumes and props for their adventure and learning to act like sailors and pirates, children also gain acting skills.

Physical Education

Physical education is promoted throughout Treasure Quest. It offers children the opportunity to participate in enjoyable physical activities, thereby promoting the concept of lifelong participation in physical activity as a pleasurable endeavor. The physical skills learned and developed in the workshop help children develop and maintain a positive self-image. The high level of physical activity in some activities, such as the Escape Course and the Island Highland Games, helps children develop and maintain physical fitness, while activities such as shipbuilding develop sensory-motor skills.

Visual Arts

Children develop visual arts knowledge and skills to express ideas imaginatively as they create pirate props, costumes, flags, patches, and other decorations. Participation in these visual arts activities also develops and expands children's aesthetic perceptions.

Language Arts and Reading

Throughout the program, children develop their listening and speaking skills as they work together to meet numerous challenges and find the hidden treasure. Word recognition is reinforced as children's ideas are recorded on facilitation boards or on the blackboard in the process of planning the shipwreck escape course. Reading skills can be expanded through activities or assignments in which children read about pirate history, sea animals, island recipes, and pirate- or sea-related fiction. Writing activities can be incorporated easily into the program activities. These activities can be selected and adapted for various ages and abilities. They might include developing a book about the adventure; writing and performing songs about the sea and islands; keeping a pirate's journal; or developing a research report on pirate history, animals that live in or near the ocean, sunken ships, sailing, costuming, etc.

History and Social Science

PLAE Scores emphasize participation skills—working individually and as a group to achieve group goals. These skills are important to the development of citizenship. They include the skills of planning, constructive criticism, self-reliance, and cooperation to develop solutions to problems. Other history and social science activities can be incorporated into *Treasure Quest*. These might include researching the history of exploration; developing a historical timeline that correlates pirate history with other notable events; investigating modernday treasure hunters; and learning about local laws and ordinances which govern the discovery and excavation of archaeological finds.

Science

Science activities can be incorporated easily into the treasure hunting curriculum. Possibilities include navigation using a compass or the sun; the study of marine animals; the origin of plant materials and their use in making fabric, paper, and cardboard; photography; the study of sound; and first aid. These activities are closely related to the Environmental Awareness activities listed on the following page.

Communication Skills

Treasure Quest helps develop a wide range of communication skills, such as speaking, listening, reading, and writing. These are used in both an individual and a group context, separately and in combination with one another.

Mathematics

Math skills can be incorporated in a number of ways. For example, clues leading to the treasure can be designed to promote geometry skills. Splitting the treasure will help children understand division, comparison, and equality. If play money is used for treasure, children can gain skills in counting money and making change. Graphs can be created throughout the workshop to measure children's reaction to two or more variables, e.g., their favorite sea animals (shark, dolphin, seal). Completed graphs can be hung as decorations. Throughout the program, calculating and problem-solving skills can be developed. How many lengths of pipe, corner sections, and sheets will be needed to make a shelter? How big should the ship be?

Cultural Awareness

Opportunities to explore other cultures can be incorporated by having children consider the lifeways of seafaring peoples as well as the various ocean resources they depend on, including animals and food.

Environmental Awareness

Treasure Quest relies on the use of recycled materials to create props and costumes, providing an important conservation concept that can be emphasized throughout the program. Children can investigate how trash and materials for recycling are handled in their city; calculate the volume of recyclable materials versus the volume of disposable refuse generated by the program each day; and compare the program's percentage of recycling to the overall city average. Children should always be encouraged to leave indoor and outdoor facilities in a better condition at the end of the program than before. To this end, clean-up and recycling activities are a central part of the program.

II. Implementing *Treasure Quest*

GOOD PLANNING IS ESSENTIAL FOR A SUCCESSFUL PLAE SCORE PROGRAM.

This section provides instructions for adapting and implementing the Treasure Quest PLAE Score to meet your program needs and site considerations.

ORGANIZING THE PLAE SCORE TEAM

Identifies the key roles in the PLAE Score Team and presents strategies for augmenting staff with volunteers or through collaboration with other professionals and organizations.

USING THIS GUIDE

Provides a brief overview of the guide's contents and how it can be used in your staff training and program operations.

ADAPTING THE PLAE SCORE

Presents a step-by-step process for adapting this PLAE Score to the particular needs of your program and facility.

GATHERING SUPPLIES

Provides directions and tips on how to gather the supplies you will need at little cost to your organization.

SETTING THE STAGE

Outlines the critical elements you will need to transform your facility into a place for fantasy adventures.

MANAGING THE PROCESS

Provides tips to ensure a smoothly operating PLAE Score program.

PLAE Scores are implemented by skilled staff members who create a fantasy experience as a context for play and learning. PLAE Scores are best implemented as a team effort. This team consists of a Program Coordinator, Playleaders, and a Resource Coordinator.

Program Coordinator

The Program Coordinator is responsible for planning, implementing, and evaluating the PLAE Score. This role may also include generating resources and financial support. During a workshop, the Program Coordinator is like the conductor of an orchestra. She or he will work as a roving staff person, promote communication among staff, and ensure smooth program operation.

Playleaders

Playleaders work directly with children to animate the environment and create the fantasy experience. They are critical to the success of the program. Their special skills in art, drama, science, and other subjects bring the PLAE Score to life. Playleaders must play a number of roles each day, including child development specialist, resource person, big brother/big sister, and social facilitator. Playleaders also serve as group facilitators and graphic recorders in the group discussions and decision making processes of PLAE Scores. These are important roles that can increase children's involvement and interest in the program and contribute to a successful workshop process. For more information on these group interaction methods, see *How To Make Meetings Work* by Michael Doyle and David Straus (New York: Berkley Publishing Group, 1976). Playleadership is a growing profession in schools and play programs around the world.

The Role of the Playleader

Resource Person

- teaches skills
- helps solve problems
- locates needed resources

Social Facilitator

- leads group discussions and decision making
- promotes relationships between:
  children
  families, children, and professionals
  staff members
  the program and the sponsoring organization
  the program and the community

Big Brother/Big Sister

- listens
- creates an accepting atmosphere
- promotes independence

Child Development Specialist

- helps children of all abilities develop intellectually, socially, physically, and emotionally
- facilitates planned and spontaneous play experiences

Resource Coordinator

Before the program begins, the Resource Coordinator gathers materials needed for the workshop through donations, recycling, general scrounging, and as a last resort—new purchases. Each day, the Resource Coordinator ensures that supplies are on-site as needed. When not collecting magical new materials, this staff person may double as a playleader.

Determining Staffing Needs

Compare the level of assistance needed by your children with your level of staffing. Depending on the age and abilities of the children, additional staff may be needed to assist with activities. Some activities require more assistance than others.

The National Association for the Education of Young Children recommends that agencies incorporate a staff/child ratio no larger than 1:18 for programs serving five- to eight-year-olds. PLAE, Inc., has found that a ratio in the range of 1:6 to 1:10 works well with an integrated group of children with and without disabilities, including several children with severe disabilities.

Strategies for Classrooms, Small Programs, and Low Budgets

In many educational and recreation programs, funding shortages and inadequate staffing levels are (unfortunately) the status quo. In classrooms or small programs, one staff member may assume the roles of the entire PLAE Score team. Nonetheless, a creative, child-directed curriculum can still be implemented. The following survival strategies are suggested:

Parent/Community Volunteers

Become a volunteer coordinator. Parent or community volunteers can serve as playleaders, each staffing a different activity. Make sure volunteers arrive for orientation well before the activities begin. Volunteers can also assist with supplies coordination. Find tasks for volunteers who cannot help during the program hours, but would be willing to help for a few hours during the evenings or weekends (e.g., preparing supplies, correcting papers, typing newsletters, preparing memos, etc.).

Team Planning/Teaching

Plan cooperatively with another staff person who will be implementing the program with a different group of participants. Team planning can take place between two teachers in charge of different classrooms or two recreation playleaders who work at different community centers. By working together, reponsibilities for planning, parent communications, gathering supplies, and program evaluation can be shared.

Specialists

Involve other specialists available at your school or through your program in developing and implementing the PLAE Score. A physical education teacher could teach activities for the Island Highland Games, a music teacher might teach nautical songs or provide a selection of sea-related music, a librarian might assist students in researching nautical history or finding pirate fiction, or an art teacher might help students design props and decorations.

Careful Planning

If you do not have sufficient staff for conducting multiple activities simultaneously, select activities that children can do with minimal supervision or assistance. You can then locate the activity which will need the most assistance in the center of the activity area so that you can assist with this activity while keeping an eye on the other activities.

Staff Training

Staff training is essential for building a successful, professional team of playleaders. At a minimum, all staff and program volunteers should be aware of the program's goals and approach. This creates a shared program vision. In addition, staff must be familiar with the curriculum prior to implementation. Providing hands-on experience with workshop activities before implementation increases staff confidence as well as their comfort level. Don't program an activity for children that the playleaders haven't tried first!

PLAE, Inc., offers PLAE Score leadership training workshops for schools and recreation agencies. The training workshop helps organizations create a professional playleadership team, implement an ongoing PLAE Score program, and create their own thematic, experiential curriculum. For more information, call 510/845-7523.

Treasure Quest is organized as a week-long, half-day curriculum. The overall curriculum structure is presented in Figure 1 (page 5). Review this figure carefully to fully understand the structure of the program and sequence of activities.

The five units that make up the Treasure Quest program are presented in Section III of this guide, "Sequence of Activities." Each unit is designed as a 3-hour session, including 15 minutes at the end for clean-up. The presentation of each unit includes the following:

Activity Flow Chart

Each unit description includes an activity flow chart (the flow chart for Unit One is on page 35). The flow charts illustrate how activities are organized in sequence during the unit. There are three types of activities represented in the flow charts:

- Large Group Activities, represented by large circles. These activities involve everyone in a single group.

- Small Group Activities, represented by small circles. These activities divide children into small groups of equal size in order to participate in a common exercise.

- PLAE Station Activities, represented by medium circles. These provide different activities simultaneously. Children may move between activities as they please, completing all of the activities within the given time frame.

The activity purpose (orientation, experience, or culmination) is indicated at the top of the flow chart. The estimated time required for each activity is indicated at the bottom of the flow chart. The flow charts do not include the time needed for set-up.

Activity Descriptions

The description for each activity in the unit includes Time Required, Type of Activity, Concept, Supplies, Preparational Activities, and Step-by-Step Instructions.

This curriculum guide should be used to introduce playleaders and other program staff to the workshop concept and process. The activity descriptions should also be used to provide step-by-step instructions for implementation of each activity. Playleaders may find it useful to organize three-ring binders containing descriptions of the activities for which they are responsible as well as any notes they may need regarding adaptations and other considerations.

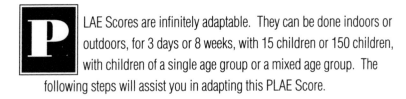

LAE Scores are infinitely adaptable. They can be done indoors or outdoors, for 3 days or 8 weeks, with 15 children or 150 children, with children of a single age group or a mixed age group. The following steps will assist you in adapting this PLAE Score.

Determine the Number of Participants

The first step in implementing a PLAE Score is to determine the number of potential participants. This figure may be based on school district quotas, your own vision of how large the program should be, or historical data from similar programs run by your agency. The program size must also be based on available facilities and funding for staff. A staff/participant ratio between 1:6 and 1:10 is recommended for play programs that integrate children with and without disabilities.

Select a Site

Choose a facility that will best suit your program's needs or develop a strategy for how best to utilize the space you have available. The major factors in site selection are its accessibility to children with disabilities (see "Involving All Children," page 6), activity requirements, and the number of participants. Indoor and outdoor spaces should comfortably accommodate participants without crowding or creating a safety hazard.

The nature of each activity determines its best location. Messy activities are often best done outside where playleaders do not need to worry about spills, dirt, and other "side effects" of the creative process. Activities with high noise levels, intense physical activity, or large space requirements are also more easily accommodated outdoors.

Research by PLAE, Inc. (1980-93), indicates that children's most memorable play experiences typically occur outdoors. Yet child-serving programs, particularly schools, structure most activities for indoors, underusing their outdoor spaces for learning. This is partly because outdoor environments are not usually designed to support program activities. Support facilities such as adequate and usable storage and outdoor sinks can help staff program the outdoor environment more easily and effectively. But even without such facilities, outdoor spaces can be utilized for a wide range of activities. Why not try reading under a tree or playing "Octopus" (described on page 65) on the playground when the weather is nice?

PLAE Scores can also be implemented indoors when preferred, or when the weather is bad or outdoor space is limited. Classroom tables and chairs should be arranged to accommodate the workshop activities, with messy activities located near a sink. To facilitate clean-up, tables should be covered with paper and painters' drop cloths should be placed on the floor. Arrange to use a gym, social hall, or other large room if an activity requires a large space or is loud and active.

Adapt the Curriculum

The PLAE Score curriculum must be adapted based on the number of hours and days available. Curriculum planning should involve your entire staff. To adapt the PLAE Score, assemble your staff and follow these steps:

Select and Brainstorm Activities

Select activities from this PLAE Score which you would like to include in your program and write them on a large piece of paper or flip chart. Brainstorm additional activities which you would like to include and write these down too. Review your list and select activities which match the needs and interests of your participants and fit the framework of your program.

PLAE Scores are based on activities which can be done successfully at a variety of skill levels. This program aspect is essential when designing a curriculum for mixed aged groups and varying ability levels. Also, remember to allow flexibility in your curriculum to incorporate children's ideas and contributions. For example, in *Treasure Quest,* children should be involved in deciding activities for the Island Highland Games.

The following three questions may be used to review the appropriateness of activities:

- Is the activity based on the interests of program participants?

- Is the activity rich enough to accommodate a wide range of abilities and disabilities?

- Is the activity age-appropriate?

Develop a Curriculum Structure

Brainstorm a list of possible themes which can be used to organize each day of the curriculum and write them on a flip chart. Create a wall-sized version of Figure 2, the planning worksheet (page 21), and choose a theme for each unit, labeling it on the worksheet. The first unit of the curriculum must provide an orientation, the middle units provide the workshop experience, and the final unit serves as the workshop culmination. The sequence of daily workshop themes should tell a story or represent a logical series of events.

Create a Daily Workshop Structure

Adapt the daily workshop structure to fit your program time frame, thinking about how your selected workshop activities can best develop the daily curriculum themes and achieve your curriculum goals. Each day or unit should begin with an orientation activity that leads into the experience activities, which develop the theme. A culminating activity should conclude each day. Write the sequence of activities and the time required for each under the appropriate daily workshop themes on your wall-sized worksheet.

	UNIT ONE *Orientation*	TIME	UNIT TWO *The Experience*	TIME	UNIT THREE *The Experience*	TIME	UNIT FOUR *The Experience*	TIME	UNIT FIVE *Culmination*	TIME
ORIENTATION An activity which introduces the day or week										
THE EXPERIENCE Cumulative or chronological activities which develop the theme										
CULMINATION ACTIVITY Activity which creates a sense of closure, results in a final product, or produces a peak experience	Clean-up	15 min	Clean-up	15 min	Clean-up	15 min	Clean-up	15 min	Clean-up	30 min
THE PRODUCT Item child creates to take home or share with others										

Figure 2: Planning Worksheet.

Organize the Activity Flow for Each Day

Using the flow chart for Unit One as an example (see page 35), create a bubble diagram to illustrate how activities will be organized each day. Each day should start with a large group orientation activity, include PLAE Station experience activities, and end in a culmination activity. Large group activities should also be used to provide an orientation between different sets of experience activities.

Develop Each Activity

For each activity, develop a one-page description that includes the time required, type of activity, concept, supplies needed, preparational activities, and step-by-step directions.

Develop a Site Set-up Plan for Each Day

Where will you hold your large group meeting and PLAE Station activities? Make a quick sketch of where the day's activities will take place.

Assemble the Customized PLAE Score

Organize your workshop structure chart, flow charts for each day, site set-up plans, and activity directions into a three-ring binder. This customized PLAE Score can be used as a staff training tool as well as your program curriculum guide.

Recycled materials from households and local businesses are a major part of PLAE Score program supplies. These materials can include rolls of paper, cardboard tubes, mirrors, bamboo poles, adhesive tape, old clothing, scrap metal, cardboard boxes—virtually anything that children can use to transform the environment and create play props. Finding these materials, organizing them for easy access, and developing new uses for them is the role of the Resource Coordinator.

An effective supplies management system is essential to the success of every PLAE Score. Following are procedures to ensure "material success."

Develop a Workshop Supplies List

Figure 3 (see pages 24 and 25) provides a comprehensive list of the materials you will need to conduct the complete curriculum of *Treasure Quest* activities. If you have developed a customized curriculum, you will need to make a similar list of supplies based on the activities you plan to conduct. In either case, you will need to determine the quantity of materials based on the number of program participants. Be sure to organize your list by unit and activity.

Obtain Supplies

Whenever possible, obtain supplies well before your program begins. There are three sources for program materials: industrial/ business donations, household donations, and (less desirable but unavoidable in some instances) purchases. If you start early, many materials can be obtained through donations. Donations can be tax-deductible if your organization has nonprofit status or your parks and recreation agency or parent/teacher organization has established a nonprofit foundation for fundraising purposes.

Industrial/Business Donations

All business operations have useful items associated with their product or service which are thrown away daily. Find out what these items are and ask the business to donate them to your organization. Figure 4 (see pages 26 and 27) provides a list of businesses and their common scrap materials. By saving these items from the scrap pile and incorporating them into your program, you are teaching children environmental awareness as well as developing a rich and inexpensive source of supplies. Be sure to follow up donations with a thank you letter. Include pictures of the children in your program using the donated supply as a special way of expressing thanks.

Household Donations

Your staff, neighbors, and the parents of participants can also be a source of program supplies. Household scraps abound and most people are more than willing to donate items which are on their way to the garbage can or simply abandoned in the garage. Send notes home with participants asking each child to bring a scrap item (but be prepared with a few extras for children who do not bring the requested supply), or provide a list of needed donations periodically and watch as supplies roll in. Figure 5 (see page 28) provides a list of common household items which can be recycled for play.

Purchases

No matter how talented the scrounger, a few items will have to be purchased. These usually include tempera paints, artist paintbrushes, scissors, and similar items. To reduce costs, try bulk purchasing or teaming up with other child-serving programs for discounts.

MASTER SUPPLIES LIST

BASIC SUPPLIES

- ☐ Matt knives (and replacement blades)
- ☐ Scissors
- ☐ Large cardboard boxes
- ☐ Duct tape
- ☐ Masking tape
- ☐ Strong string or cord
- ☐ Staple gun and staples
- ☐ Tempera paint in assorted colors
- ☐ Containers for paint: 32 oz. plastic yogurt containers, cut-down milk cartons, etc.
- ☐ Paintbrushes: large, medium, and small
- ☐ Fabric dye in assorted colors
- ☐ Plastic buckets for dye
- ☐ Rubberbands
- ☐ Pencils (with erasers)
- ☐ Pencil sharpeners
- ☐ Marking pens (water-based, assorted colors)
- ☐ Black fine-tip felt marking pens
- ☐ Old newspapers (to cover work surfaces)
- ☐ PVC Pipe Building System (see "Props and Patterns," page 98)
- ☐ Sheets

- ☐ Tape players
- ☐ Taped seafaring music and sound effects
- ☐ Decorations for the meeting spaces, PLAE Stations, etc.: signs, streamers, etc.
- ☐ Large worktables
- ☐ Imagination and enthusiasm!

In addition to the basic supplies, you will need the following supplies for specific activities:

TREASURE QUEST!

- ☐ Newsprint for the giant sign up scrolls
- ☐ Cardboard facilitation board (approx. 3 feet by 6 feet)

TELESCOPES

- ☐ Cardboard tubes (paper towel rolls)
- ☐ Plastic food wrap (enough for two 5-inch squares per child)
- ☐ Wrapping paper (shiny) to cover tubes
- ☐ Stickers, etc. for telescope decorations
- ☐ Invisible plastic mending tape

FLAGS

- ☐ 36-inch bamboo garden stakes (one per child)

BILLOWING SAILS

- ☐ 10- to 12-foot poles (one per mast)
- ☐ 6-foot dowels or bamboo garden stakes (one per mast)
- ☐ Wooden stands for poles (one per mast)
- ☐ 1/2-inch rope (large roll)

SAILING SONGS

- ☐ Guitar or other musical instrument
- ☐ Music (enough copies of each song for every child). These can be collated to form a "Treasure Quest Songbook"

SHIPWRECK!

- ☐ Ghost costume for an adult

THE ESCAPE COURSE

The supplies for the escape courses can be extremely varied. The idea is to provide children with a number of different materials. This will allow them to use their imaginations to build an obstacle course that represents the many dangers they must face as they escape from their ship to the island. The following list suggests materials that might be included in this activity. Other materials may also be included:

- ☐ Cardboard drums
- ☐ Nets
- ☐ Balance beams
- ☐ Tumbling mats
- ☐ Rope
- ☐ Water hoses
- ☐ Sprinkler attachments
- ☐ Sheets of plastic
- ☐ Plastic milk crates
- ☐ Crepe paper
- ☐ Wooden stakes

VILLAGE BUILDING

- ☐ Materials from wrecked ship

Figure 3: Comprehensive Supplies List for Treasure Quest.

VILLAGE IDENTITY

☐ Pillow cases

☐ Safety pins

☐ 36-inch bamboo garden stakes

☐ Large pieces of newsprint

☐ Large pieces of cardboard

ISLAND EATS

☐ Small paper bowls

☐ Measuring spoons: tablespoons, 1/2 teaspoons

☐ Forks

☐ Paper plates

☐ Small containers (e.g., clean cottage cheese cartons to distribute ingredients to sub-stations, if needed)

☐ Peanut butter

☐ Instant nonfat dry milk

☐ Raisins

☐ Honey

☐ Coconut

GHOST STORIES

The games in this section have been selected because they promote community spirit and do not require any special equipment. Any game can be adapted to a pirate theme and used during this session. The games included here were adapted from *The New Games Book* (New York: Dolphin Books, 1976) and *More New Games* (New York: Dolphin Books, 1981). If competitive games are used, emphasize "personal best" over competing with others and participating rather than winning.

AWARDS CEREMONY

☐ Award certificates (one per child; see "Props and Patterns," page 89)

ARRGH!

☐ Pirate costume for an adult

PIRATE HATS

☐ White poster board

☐ Black poster board

☐ Hat pattern (see "Props and Patterns," page 95)

EYE PATCHES

☐ Black vinyl

☐ Elastic thread

BANDANAS

☐ Clothesline

☐ Clothespins or safety pins

TREASURE BOXES

☐ Shoeboxes (one per child)

☐ Fabric to cover boxes

☐ White glue

☐ Glue containers: 16 oz. plastic containers, pint milk cartons, cottage cheese containers, etc.

☐ Glue brushes

☐ Decorations for treasure boxes: buttons, stickers, glitter, etc.

PIRATE TRAINING

☐ Strong rope, in approximately 25-foot lengths (two lengths per group)

☐ Poles, at least 6-1/2 feet in length

TREASURE HUNTING TOOLS

☐ Bottles

☐ Colored paper (a different color for each team)

☐ Compasses

☐ Site maps

☐ Code books (see "PLAE Props and Patterns," page 91)

☐ Treasure chests (one per team)

☐ Treasure! (costume jewelry, etc.)

☐ Treasure boxes (made by children in the previous unit)

☐ Pirate costumes (made by children in the previous unit)

Figure 3, continued: Comprehensive Supplies List for Treasure Quest.

BUSINESS	ITEMS	BUSINESS	ITEMS	BUSINESS	ITEMS
AIRLINES	Plastic cups (used OK), packing boxes	CHURCHES	Old candles	DRUG STORES	Small plastic bottles, crayons, other school supplies
ARCHITECTS	Blueprints and blueprint paper, slide rules, and other tools	CONTAINER COMPANIES	Large cardboard sheets, damaged containers— sturdy and uniform size	ELECTRIC POWER COMPANIES	Wire, large spools, assorted packing materials
ART SUPPLY STORES, STATIONERY STORES	Leftover or damaged paper or stock (e.g., paint, pencils, paper clips, staplers, markers, etc.)	CONTRACTORS, LUMBER COMPANIES	Lumber, pipes, wire, tiles, wallpaper, linoleum, molding wood, wood curls, concrete, etc.	FURNITURE STORES AND FACTORIES	Large packing boxes, packing material, fabric swatches and scraps
BILLBOARD COMPANIES	Pieces of billboards to use as posters, wall coverings, etc.	DEPARTMENT STORES	Stocking boxes, lingerie boxes, fabric swatches, rug pieces, corrugated packing cardboard, packing boxes from appliances and pianos, styrofoam packing material, decorative displays, old posters and business forms, shoeboxes, envelopes, etc.	GARMENT FACTORIES, CLOTHING FIRMS	Buttons, decorative tape, ribbon, yarn, trim, spools, fasteners, fabric scraps, etc.
BUILDING SUPPLY COMPANIES	Wood and lumber, tiles, wallpaper books, color samples, leftover formica, damaged bricks, doweling			GIFT SHOPS, BOUTIQUES	Candles, packing boxes, styrofoam packing materials, wrapping paper, ribbon, etc.
BOTTLING FIRMS	Bottle caps, large cardboard tubes	DIME STORES	Boxes, leftover or damaged crayons, leftover toys, school supplies, etc.	GROCERY STORES, SUPERMARKETS, OUTDOOR MARKETS	Cartons, packing materials, fruit crates, large cardboard and materials from displays

Figure 4: Local Business Materials Scrounge List.

BUSINESS	ITEMS	BUSINESS	ITEMS	BUSINESS	ITEMS
Grocery Stores, Supermarkets, Outdoor Markets (cont.)	Discarded display racks, styrofoam fruit trays, baskets of any sort	**Offices (cont.)**	Pencils and erasers, office furniture, file cabinets, lamps, typewriters, envelopes, manila file folders, large envelopes (used OK)	**Repair Shops**	Unclaimed appliances (preferably working), record players, typewriters, sewing machines, clocks, fans, etc.
Hardware Stores	Sample hardware books, sample tile charts, linoleum samples, rope, chain, wood, molding strips, etc.	**Paint Stores**	Leftover paint samples, sample books, wallpaper books, rolls of wallpaper, tiles, linoleum, etc.	**Restaurants, Ice Cream Stores**	Ice cream containers, corks, boxes and cartons, bottle caps
Hospitals, Hotels	Clean, discarded sheets and pillowcases	**Paper Companies, Printing Companies**	Endcuts, damaged paper, posters (blank on one side) —any size, weight, or color	**Rug Companies**	Leftovers or scraps, sample swatches, and carpet pieces
Leather Craft Companies (pocketbook, belt, & shoe makers)	Scraps of leather and lacings	**Phone Company**	Colored wires, old telephones, large spools	**Textile Companies, Upholsterers, Tailors**	Color samples, scraps, or pieces of material, spools, buttons, cord, string, etc.
Newspapers	Large rolls of paper for graphic recording	**Plastic Companies**	Trimmings, cuttings, tubing, scrap plastic, and Plexiglass	**Tile and Ceramic Companies**	Leftover damaged tile
Offices	Discontinued business forms and posters (anything blank on one side)	**Plumbers, Plumbing Supplies**	Wires, pipes, tile scraps, and linoleum	**Toy Stores**	Leftovers, damaged products, packing materials, boxes, etc.

Figure 4, continued: Local Business Materials Scrounge List.

HOUSEHOLD ITEMS

FOOD-RELATED ITEMS

- ☐ Egg cartons
- ☐ Plastic containers (margarine tubs, bleach bottles, squeeze bottles, etc.)
- ☐ Aluminum pie tins
- ☐ Straws
- ☐ Juice cans
- ☐ Meat and produce trays
- ☐ Orange crates
- ☐ Strawberry boxes and baskets
- ☐ Bottle caps
- ☐ Corks
- ☐ Popsicle sticks
- ☐ Kitchen utensils

STATIONERY SUPPLIES

- ☐ Old greeting cards
- ☐ Wrapping paper
- ☐ Rubber bands
- ☐ Envelopes
- ☐ Folders (new and used)
- ☐ Rulers, yardsticks, and tape measures
- ☐ Crayons
- ☐ Tape

- ☐ Carbon paper
- ☐ Corrugated paper and cardboard
- ☐ Stencils and paper
- ☐ All sorts of paper products (crepe paper, used or new paper cups and plates, tissue paper, contact paper, etc.)
- ☐ Paste and glue
- ☐ Staplers, staples, and paper clips
- ☐ Pencils and pens
- ☐ Scissors and paper cutters
- ☐ Typewriters

CLOTHING, ETC.

- ☐ Mardi Gras beads and trinkets
- ☐ Coat hangers
- ☐ Old clothes (dresses, socks, costumes)
- ☐ Old stockings
- ☐ Hats
- ☐ Jewelry
- ☐ Eyeglasses

SEWING SUPPLIES

- ☐ Sewing machines
- ☐ Fabric and felt
- ☐ Spools

- ☐ Yarn, string, rope
- ☐ Buttons
- ☐ Ribbon

PACKING MATERIALS

- ☐ Cardboard tubes
- ☐ Styrofoam packing material
- ☐ Sturdy boxes
- ☐ Large appliance boxes or crates

LUMBER/HARDWARE, ETC.

- ☐ Plumbing pipe
- ☐ Rug and carpet pieces
- ☐ Wood scraps and pieces
- ☐ Nails and screws
- ☐ Boards
- ☐ Bricks and concrete blocks
- ☐ Wallpaper
- ☐ Wire screens and chicken wire
- ☐ Leftover paint
- ☐ Tiles and linoleum
- ☐ Tools (hammers, saws, screwdrivers, etc.)

ETC.

- ☐ Paper bags and plastic bags
- ☐ Broken appliances with moving parts (e.g., clocks, radios, fans, etc.)
- ☐ Electronic equipment scraps
- ☐ Old toothbrushes
- ☐ Magazines
- ☐ Candles and wax
- ☐ Maps
- ☐ Durable containers
- ☐ Foam rubber
- ☐ Old furniture (especially desks, lamps, and shelves)
- ☐ Pillows and cushions
- ☐ Baskets
- ☐ Books (especially children's books)
- ☐ Natural and found objects (e.g., flat stones, pine cones, feathers, driftwood, rice, beans, etc.)
- ☐ Records, record players
- ☐ Musical instruments
- ☐ Games and puzzles
- ☐ Clay
- ☐ Toys (new or old)

Figure 5: Household Materials Scrounge List.

Develop a Supplies Resource Directory

Create a form or computer database to track sources of donations or inexpensive suppliers of commonly purchased items. Keep these in a binder or file to systematize resource collection.

Develop a Storage System

Be sure to have an effective storage program ready to handle the donated and purchased items once they find their way to your door. Items must be stored for convenient use. If they are not, playleaders will not use them.

A set of sturdy cardboard boxes (e.g., banker's boxes or copy paper boxes) are a good—and often free—solution for storing specific activity supplies. Label each box with the workshop name and the name of the activity, storing all of the supplies needed for each activity in one or more labeled boxes. These boxes can be easily stored and then transported to a PLAE Station when needed.

A separate box can be used to store materials and tools that are used for every workshop. These include playleader aprons or fanny packs for carrying supplies, scissors, transparent tape, masking tape, duct tape, glue, string, staple guns, matt knives, small handtools, and a first aid kit.

Develop New Ideas for Found Materials

Sooner or later it will happen to you. While scrounging for supplies for a specific activity, you will come across unrelated but interesting and seemingly useful free material. Take this donation, even if you are not immediately sure how you will use it. Look through craft books for ideas or let children develop a way of incorporating the material into the PLAE Score.

Create Community Reuse Solutions

Some communities have developed centralized spaces for collecting scrap materials from businesses and individuals for use in play and education programs. One such place is the East Bay Depot for Creative Reuse in Oakland, CA (1027 60th Street, Oakland, CA 94608, 510/547-6470). Paid and volunteer staff collect scrap materials at the center; teachers and playleaders pick up needed items by the bagful for a nominal fee or membership. A similar strategy can be implemented in a school, recreation agency, or on a citywide basis.

Setting the stage is a method used by playleaders to engage children, capture their imagination, and make them eager to experience the activities which follow. Playleaders should plan for setting the stage while developing the curriculum. In most education and recreation programs, waiting time is dead time. In a PLAE workshop, the fun begins as soon as the first child arrives.

Children's first impressions are the most important. The environment should scream, "You have now entered the world of *Treasure Quest!* You are now a treasure hunter and this is your ship!"

Following are some methods that can be used to set the stage for *Treasure Quest.*

Costumes

Playleaders can set the stage themselves by becoming embodiments of the theme. For *Treasure Quest,* try being a pirate or a ship's captain. Children can also express themselves and bring the theme to life through costumes. Creating costumes is always a good workshop activity.

Music

Music is unequaled in evoking memories and creating the spirit of a setting. How many of us associate a special event or time in life with a particular song? Playing recorded seafaring music as children assemble for the workshop will help create an exciting atmosphere.

Signs and Displays

Large signs, posters, and displays add to the stage set and attract attention to the program. Staff or children should create a few large signs prior to the program. Some suggestions include "Wanted: Treasure Hunters!" or other "join the crew" messages, "Map for Lost Treasure Discovered," or "Beware of Pirates!" Invent your own! As activities are completed, any new products should be added to the stage set to create a pirate-like atmosphere. These can include group brainstorming results recorded on large sheets of paper, graphs of favorite sea animals, collections of sailing props, and displays of pirate books or nautical posters.

Decorations

The type of decorations used depends on the configuration of the particular play environment. The important thing is to create a significant presence in the workshop location. Use plenty of color and strive for a larger-than-life impact. Wallpaper or curtains in an old sailing theme can be used to enclose an area (e.g., the supply shed or the front of the recreation center) or large pieces of cardboard can form temporary walls for decoration. How about a poster made from original illustrations of Robert Louis Stevenson's *Treasure Island?* A large pirate facade with the face cut out so a child can peek through? A parrot who talks? Giant sailor dolls created out of stuffed clothes? Decorations can be created by children and staff before and during the workshop. They are limited only by your imagination and your ability to scrounge, borrow, and transform.

Demonstrations

Demonstrations can be used to introduce children to the workshop as they arrive. They should be fast and fun and should involve the children as active participants. Demonstrations should begin about 10 minutes before the scheduled workshop and continue until most of the children have arrived. Demonstrations should not involve too much instruction on the part of playleaders or too much personal disclosure on the part of children. As more children arrive at the site, they should be able to join the fun without disrupting the activity.

Some suggestions:

- *Sailor Skills.* Teach children basic nautical skills, such as knot tying, how to tell time by the sun, and how to use a compass.

- *Island Studies.* Study the weather (make a stuffed cloud) and island life (plants, insects, and animals). Plant some vegetable seeds on the island in case you run out of food.

- *Fishing Booth.* Paint the numbers 1-10 on the bottom of 25 to 30 plastic fish. Then fill a large wading pool with water, attach a wire loop to the fish mouths, and deposit the fish in the water. Children catch the fish with a rod (dowel with a length of string on one end and a plastic shower curtain hook attached to the string). Who can accumulate the most points before the workshop begins?

- *Flag Messages.* Teach children how to send flag messages to fellow islanders who live far away.

- *Pirate Games.* Adapt games to a pirate theme and play them.

- *Model Ships.* Do a fast craft activity like building model ships out of styrofoam hamburger containers (1/2 container per ship), decorating them with marking pens.

- *Snack on Oranges.* Prevent scurvy by having children peel and eat oranges.

The following tips will help ensure that your PLAE Score runs as smoothly as possible:

Activity Set-up

Allow time for staff to set up activities each day before children arrive.

Team Orientation Meeting

Before the workshop each day, meet with staff to review upcoming activities, timing, and leadership roles. Provide each staff member with a copy of the activity flow chart for that day. Staff assignments can be written in each bubble on the flow chart. The flow chart will serve as a quick reference for activity plans and responsibilities throughout the day.

Workshop Documentation

Photograph or videotape your workshop! These visual records will prove invaluable for fundraising, public awareness, and future staff training.

Clean-up Activities

Involve children in cleaning up the workshop activities each day. This helps avoid staff burnout and develops responsibility in children.

Team Debriefing

At the end of each day, meet briefly with staff to discuss the workshop and identify those elements that worked well and those that need improvement. Take notes and modify your workshop accordingly.

Program Evaluation

Provide an opportunity for staff, parents, and children to evaluate the workshop program through meetings or written evaluation. Incorporate suggestions for improvement in the curriculum.

III. Sequence of Activities

THIS SECTION PRESENTS THE FIVE UNITS THAT MAKE UP THE COMPLETE *TREASURE QUEST PLAE SCORE.*

Before launching into the activities, be sure you have reviewed the first two sections of this book and completed all of the necessary preparations to ensure success on your island adventure.

HAVE FUN!

Setting the Stage

The treasure hunting fun begins when the first child arrives. Be sure to set the stage for the PLAE Score well in advance so that you have plenty of time to welcome new arrivals. See "Setting the Stage," page 30, for ideas on how to create an exciting and inviting treasure hunting atmosphere. Once all of the participants have arrived, go ahead with the first activity.

A Note Regarding Activity Descriptions

Many of the activity descriptions include brief scripts to provide prompts for addressing children and advancing the storyline. These can be helpful for training young staff members and volunteers, but should be elaborated upon, altered, and eventually discarded as you improvise and create your own seafaring style.

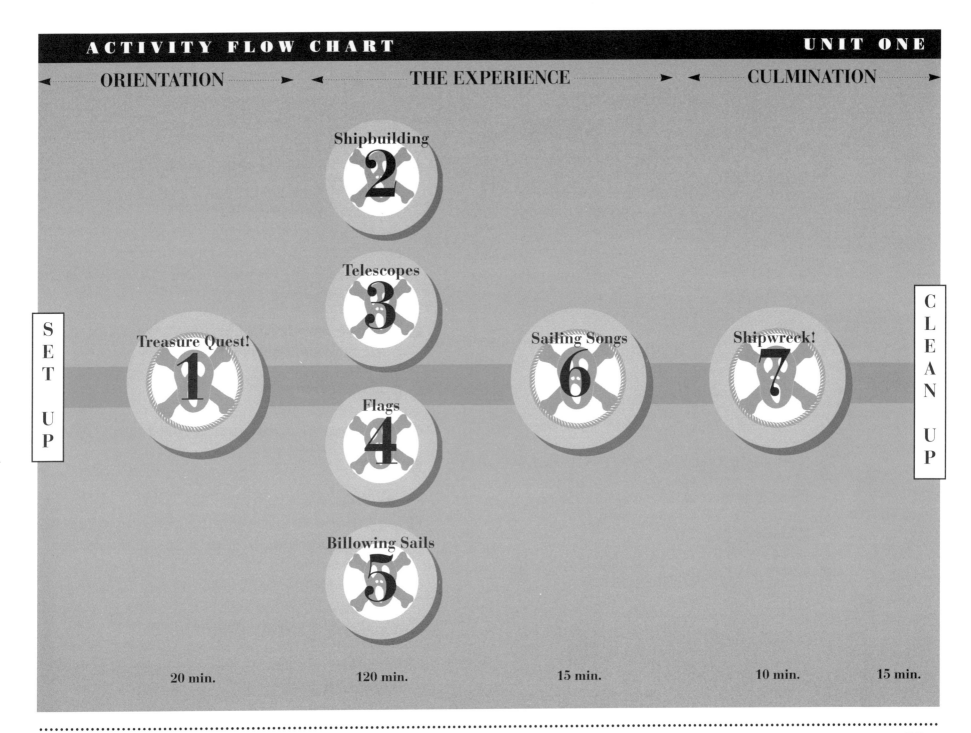

ORIENTATION   THE EXPERIENCE   CULMINATION

SET UP

Shipbuilding
2

Telescopes
3

Treasure Quest!
1

Flags
4

Sailing Songs
6

Shipwreck!
7

Billowing Sails
5

CLEAN UP

20 min.   120 min.   15 min.   10 min.   15 min.

Activity 1: Treasure Quest!

Time Required: *20 minutes*

Type of Activity: *Orientation; Large Group*

Concept:
Children sign up for the treasure hunting adventure and are told the story of the buried treasure.

Supplies:
- Decorations for the meeting space: signs, streamers, etc.

- Newsprint for the giant sign-up scroll(s)

- "Treasure Hunters" banner for scroll (see "Props and Patterns," page 98)

- Black fine-tip felt marking pens

- Cardboard facilitation board (approximately 3 feet by 6 feet)

- Matt knives

- Scissors

- Duct tape

- Strong string or cord

- Staple gun and staples

Preparational Activities:

❶ *Prior to Unit One:* Prepare the sign-up scroll(s) by cutting a piece of newsprint the size of the cardboard facilitation board. The edges of the paper can be torn or burned to make the scrolls look old and the "Treasure Hunters" banner can be placed at the top (see page 98). The paper can then be stapled to the cardboard with a staple gun. The sign-up board(s) can be hung at the meeting site (at a height appropriate for the children) or they can be held by leaders.

❷ Divide the playleaders into groups, with a ship's captain and a first mate in each. There should be a group and a scroll for every 15 to 20 children. The captain's and first mate's name should be written at the top of their scroll.

❸ Assign a playleader to introduce the activity and tell the story.

❹ *Before You Begin:* Decorate the large group meeting area as desired.

Step-by-Step:

❶ As children arrive, instruct them to sign up as crewmembers on one of the ship's logs (sign-up scrolls). The captain and first mate of each ship can help children sign up on their ship's scroll, and should introduce themselves to their crew. They can also help introduce crew members to each other as they sign aboard. Direct the children so that each ship has an equal number of crewmembers (15 to 20 per ship).

Once the crews have formed, they should all sit together to hear the story of *Treasure Quest.*

❷ One leader tells the story:

"Ahoy, maties! Welcome aboard. We're about to embark on a quest for buried treasure!

"According to legend, a Spanish galleon loaded with treasure was taken by pirates many years ago off the shores of a distant isle. One pirate, Long John Silver, who was very greedy, took more treasure than he could carry. He found a secret spot on the island and buried the treasure there so he could return for it later.

"On his journey home he was a caught in a great storm that sank his ship and took his life. The only thing that survived the wreck was the bottle in which Long John had put the map showing where he buried the treasure. That bottle washed ashore last week and WE now have the map showing where the hidden treasure is buried!

"We're so glad you could all make it for the voyage. We're going to need every hand on deck if we're to make it across the sea and find the buried treasure. But first, we're going to need to build a ship and make the equipment we'll need for our trip. Best o' luck mates, and beware of the ghost of Long John Silver!"

Activity 2:   Shipbuilding

Time Required: *2 hours (conducted simultaneously with Activities 3, 4, and 5)*

Type of Activity: *The Experience; PLAE Station (1 of 4)*

Concept:
Children construct a ship for their treasure hunting adventure.

Supplies:
- Large cardboard boxes

- Matt knives

- Masking tape

- Duct tape

- Scissors

- Tempera paint in assorted colors

- Containers for paint: 32 oz. plastic yogurt containers, cut-down milk cartons, etc.

- Paintbrushes: large, medium, and small

- PVC Pipe Building System (see "Props and Patterns," page 97)

- Large worktable

Preparational Activities:

1 *Prior to Unit One:* Select a location for the PLAE Station that is suitable for constructing the ship. A raised platform, a play structure, or a similar feature can provide a "foundation" for the ship. Be creative and be sure that PLAE Stations are separate enough to avoid distraction.

2 Assign two playleaders to conduct the activity.

3 *Before You Begin:* Arrange the cardboard boxes at the activity site. Organize paint (poured into individual paint containers) and paintbrushes on the worktable.

4 During the activity, leaders should carry a matt knife, masking tape, duct tape, and scissors to assist children in construction. A utility apron is useful for this (see "Props and Patterns," page 96).

5 Leaders for this activity need not worry about making the mast and sails for the ship (see Activity 5), but should plan a space for it to be put when the ship is under construction.

6 Decorate the PLAE Station.

Step-by-Step:

❶ Playleaders explain to their crew that they are to build a ship using the cardboard boxes, sheets, and PVC Pipe Building System. Use the PVC pipes as the structure and the cardboard and sheets as the skin. The children arrange and tape the boxes (with assistance from the leaders) in the configuration of a ship. A number of boxes should be organized to serve as individual staterooms for the children. Staterooms should be arranged so that the children can enter and exit easily. Any cutting required to create doors and portholes should be done by the leaders, using matt knives. Matt knives should never be used by children.

❷ Each child can paint the inside and outside of their stateroom and other parts of the ship using the tempera paints.

❸ While the ship is being built, some children may wish to go to one of the other PLAE Stations that are being operated simultaneously.

❹ Once the sails are complete (see Activity 5), they can be installed on the ship. The children can also hang their flags (see Activity 4) on the inside or outside of their staterooms.

Activity 3:   Telescopes

Time Required: *2 hours (conducted simultaneously with activities 2, 4, and 5)*

Type of Activity: *The Experience; PLAE Station (1 of 4)*

Concept:
Children create telescopes as props for their sailing adventure.

Supplies:

- Cardboard tubes (paper towel rolls; one per child)

- Plastic food wrap (enough for two 5-inch squares per child)

- Wrapping paper (shiny) to cover tubes

- Stickers, etc. for telescope decorations

- Invisible plastic mending tape

- Scissors

- Ink pens

- Decorations for the PLAE Station

- 2 large worktables

Preparational Activities:

❶ *Prior to Unit One:* Assign playleaders to conduct the activity.

❷ *Before You Begin:* Arrange supplies on the worktable(s).

❸ Decorate the PLAE Station.

Step-by-Step:

❶ As children arrive at the PLAE Station, give each a cardboard tube and show them how to install (tape) a lens (a piece of plastic wrap) on each end of their telescope.

❷ Once the plastic is on, children cut wrapping paper to fit the length of their tube.

❸ The children wrap the paper around their tube and tape it with invisible plastic mending tape. Stickers or other decorations may be added to the telescope as desired.

❹ Each child can then use an ink pen to identify his or her telescope.

❺ Children may then go to one of the other PLAE Stations that are being operated simultaneously.

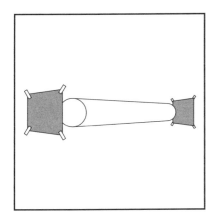

Tape a piece of plastic over the ends of a cardboard tube.

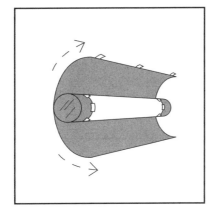

Wrap the tube in paper.

Decorate with marking pens, stickers, and other materials.

Activity 4: Flags

Time Required: *2 hours (conducted simultaneously with activities 2, 3, and 5)*

Type of Activity: *The Experience; PLAE Station (1 of 4)*

Concept:
Children create flags as props for their sailing adventure.

Supplies:
- 36-inch bamboo garden stakes (one per child)

- Sheets (enough to make a 3-foot by 2-foot flag for each child)

- Fabric dye in assorted colors

- Plastic buckets for dye

- Rubberbands

- Tempera paints in assorted colors

- Containers for paint

- Paintbrushes: medium and small

- Scissors

- String

- Masking tape

- Large worktables (at least two).

- Cardboard (enough to lay "flags" on for painting and drying)

- Decorations for the PLAE Station

Preparational Activities:

1 *Prior to Unit One:* Assign two playleaders to conduct the activity.

2 Cut the sheets into pieces of approximately 3 feet by 2 feet.

3 *Before You Begin:* Arrange the sheets, bamboo stakes, string, masking tape, and rubberbands on one of the worktables.

4 On the second worktable, arrange the paint (in individual containers) and paintbrushes.

5 Mix the dye in the buckets and place them near the painting table.

6 Set up an area where the flags can be painted and/or dried.

7 Decorate the PLAE Station.

Step-by-Step:

❶ As children arrive at the PLAE Station, give each a flag that they may decorate by dyeing and/or painting.

❷ Children can use the scissors to cut their flag into a different shape, if they desire. They can then either dye their flag one color, tie-dye their flag many colors, paint a design on their flag, or any combination of these.

❸ While the flags are drying, children may go to one of the other PLAE Stations that are being operated simultaneously.

❹ When the flags are dry, the playleader can help the children mount their flags on sticks. Using scissors, the playleader cuts three holes on one side of the flag. The children can then put strings through the holes and tie their flag to a stick. The strings can be secured with masking tape if necessary.

FLAGS

Activity 5:   Billowing Sails

Time Required: *2 hours (conducted simultaneously with activities 2, 3, and 4)*

Type of Activity: *The Experience; PLAE Station (1 of 4)*

Concept:
Children create sails for their treasure hunting ship.

Supplies:
- Sheets (at least one per mast)

- 10- to 12-foot poles (at least two)

- 6-foot dowels or bamboo garden stakes (one per mast)

- Wooden stands for poles (one per mast)

- 1/2-inch rope (large roll)

- String

- Tempera paint in assorted colors

- Paint containers

- Paintbrushes: large and medium

- Scissors

- Cardboard (enough to lay sheets on for painting and drying)

- Large worktable(s)

- Decorations for the PLAE Station

Preparational Activities:

1 *Prior to Unit One:* Assign playleaders to conduct the activity.

2 Cut the sheets into sail shapes (triangular).

3 Construct wooden stands which will securely hold the poles during the workshop. It is important that they be tested with the sails hung prior to Unit One.

4 Build the masts. Use a long pole as the mast. Using the rope, tie a 6-foot bamboo stake perpendicularly to the mast, making the boom. It should be located about a third of the way up the mast so that the sail will fit between the top of the mast and the boom.

5 *Before You Begin:* Arrange supplies at the PLAE Station: paint and paintbrushes on the worktable, and sheets cut into sail shapes on the cardboard.

6 Decorate the PLAE Station.

Step-by-Step:

❶ As children arrive at the PLAE Station, they should be given a paintbrush and instructed to paint the sails.

❷ As the sails are drying, children may go to one of the other PLAE Stations that are being operated simultaneously.

❸ When the sails are painted and dried, the masts can be placed on the ground and the children can help tie the sails to them using the string. Playleaders can cut holes along the sails' edges. The children can then put string through the holes and tie the sail to the mast and boom.

❹ When the sails are attached, the masts can be placed in their stands and put on the ship (see Activity 2). Additional rope can be used to tie down and brace the mast if necessary.

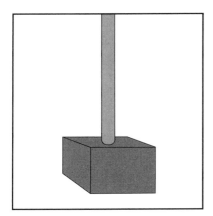

Find or make a stand to securely hold the masts in position.

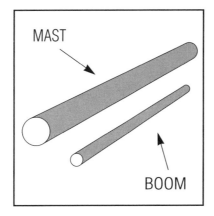

Use the large pole as the mast and a dowel or bamboo garden stake as the boom.

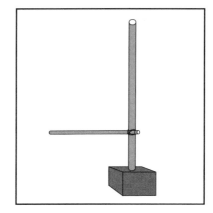

Tie the boom to the mast pole. It should be a third of the way up the mast and perpendicular to it.

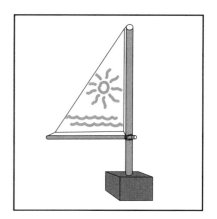

Attach decorated sheets as the sails.

Activity 6:   Sailing Songs

Time Required: *15 minutes*

Type of Activity: *The Experience; Large Group*

Concept:
Children sing sailing songs to develop the theme.

Supplies:
• Guitar or other musical instrument

• Music (enough copies of each song for every child)—these can be collated to form a "Treasure Quest Songbook"

• Decorations for the large group meeting area

Preparational Activities:
❶ *Prior to Unit One:* Assign a playleader to lead the songs and play the guitar. It can be one playleader who does this or more, depending on skills.

❷ Locate children's music with a mariner flavor that will help develop the workshop theme. Suggestions: *Puff the Magic Dragon, Yellow Submarine, Row Row Row Your Boat, My Bonnie Lies over the Ocean*, etc. Prepare copies of each song with the lyrics in large, bold print.

❸ *Before You Begin:* Decorate the large group meeting area as desired.

Step-by-Step:
❶ Ask the children to sit in a large group (perhaps around or on the ship) and pass out the music.

❷ Introduce the songs and encourage everyone to join in, telling the children how sailors sang on their ships during the long days they spent traveling between ports. Other leaders should sit with the crew and sing too.

SING-ALONG

Activity 7:   Shipwreck!

Time Required: *10 minutes*

Type of Activity: *Culmination; Large Group*

Concept:
A ghost warns the treasure hunters that they are in danger.

Supplies:
- Ghost costume for an adult

Preparational Activities:

1 *Prior to Unit One:* Assign a playleader to portray the ghost of Long John Silver.

2 He or she should develop a ghost costume prior to the workshop. It can consist of a sheet with eye holes, an eye patch, and a bandana. Use your imagination!

3 *Before You Begin:* As the children gather for songs, the chosen playleader slips away to put on his or her costume.

Step-by-Step:

1 The ghost's entrance and speech provide the culmination to Unit One's activities and set the stage for Unit Two's "Escape Course."

2 When the children are together in a large group (see Activity 6), the ghost enters from out of nowhere:

"Avast, yon landlubbers! So ye thinks ye can sail ta my secret island and steal what is rightfully mine! Well, I'm the ghost of Long John Silver and I've come fer ta warn ye young lads and lasses—BEWARE! The seas are rough and the future dark for those who dare draw near ta my treasure. Ye're in danger already. Be kind ta yerselves and cancel yer voyage while ye still have a chance. Or the curse of the ghost of Long John Silver will weigh heavily upon ye and fill yer passage with danger and despair. And when ye're goin' down fer the third time ta sleep with the fishes ferever, don't say Long John didn't warn ye!"

3 The ghost exits.

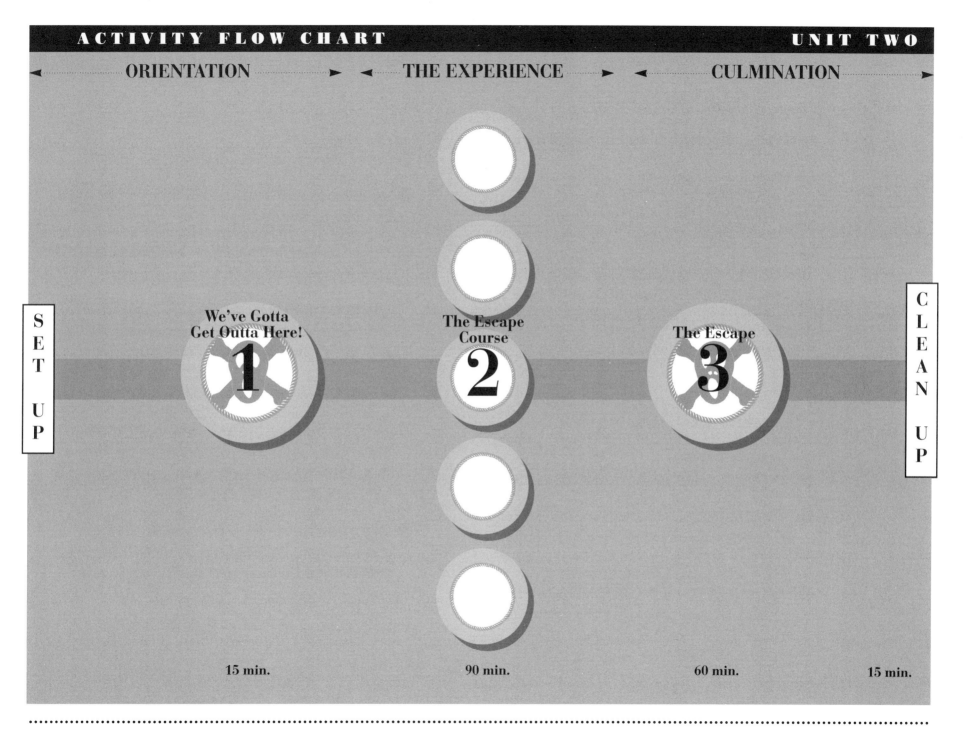

ORIENTATION THE EXPERIENCE CULMINATION

SET UP

We've Gotta Get Outta Here! 1

The Escape Course 2

The Escape 3

CLEAN UP

15 min. 90 min. 60 min. 15 min.

Activity 1:   We've Gotta Get Outta Here!

Time Required: *15 minutes*

Type of Activity: *Orientation; Large Group*

Concept:
Playleaders hold a large group meeting to orient children to the continuing workshop story and prepare them for the activities of Unit Two.

Supplies:
- Decorations for the PLAE Station: signs, streamers, etc.

- Tape player

- Taped storm sounds (e.g., wind, rain, thunder, etc.)

Preparational Activities:
❶ *Prior to Unit Two:* Assign a playleader to introduce the activity.

❷ Determine the number of small groups into which the large group will divide for Activity 2. Assign at least one playleader to lead each small group.

❸ *Before You Begin:* Decorate the PLAE Station with themes for the day (e.g., S.O.S., rain clouds, shark heads and fins made of cardboard, lightning bolts, etc.).

Step-by-Step:
❶ Greet the children as they arrive and gather them around the ship.

❷ Play the recorded storm sounds and ask the children to pretend they are being tossed by the wind and waves.

❸ The playleader introducing the activity tells the children that their ship is sinking in a storm and that they need to find a way to escape:

"It seems we should have heeded the warning of the ghost of Long John Silver! Our ship has been caught in a terrible storm and we're taking on water quickly! We won't be able to stay afloat much longer. Luckily, we're very close to the shores of an island. We need to find some way to escape and make our way to the island or our voyage will be a failure!

"We're going to need everyone's help! Now we're going to break up into groups and figure out some way to escape before the ship goes under. We don't have long! And be careful! Few have survived the shark-filled waters and jagged rocks surrounding the island!"

❹ Children can be divided into equal-sized groups by counting off or use of a similar method. The playleaders for each small group in Activity 2 should lead the appropriate number of children to their group's area.

Activity 2:   **The Escape Course**

Time Required: *90 minutes*

Type of Activity: *The Experience; Small Groups*

Concept:
Children create an escape course to simulate their escape from the sinking ship.

Supplies:
The supplies for the escape course can be extremely varied. The idea is to provide the children with a number of different materials. This will allow them to use their imaginations to build an obstacle course that represents the many dangers they must face as they escape from their ship to the island. The following list suggests materials that might be included in this activity. Other materials may also be included.

- Large cardboard boxes

- Cardboard drums

- Nets

- Balance beams

- Tumbling mats

- Sheets

- String

- Rope

- Scissors (adult)

- Matt knives

- Tempera paints in assorted colors

- Water hoses

- Sprinkler attachments

- Sheets of plastic

- Plastic milk crates

- Paint containers

- Paintbrushes: large and medium

- Crepe paper

- Wooden stakes

- Large worktables (one for each small group)

- Tape players

- Sound effect tapes

Preparational Activities:

❶ *Prior to Unit Two:* Identify a large space where the children can create their escape course. This space may be entirely flat or may contain items or obstacles (walls, sand pits, play equipment, etc.) that can be integrated into an obstacle course. Divide the large area into smaller areas so that each small group will be responsible for one part of the overall course.

❷ Demarcate each of the small group areas using signs and/or crepe paper "ropes."

❸ Define general themes for each part of the escape course (e.g., escaping from the ship, swimming through the sharks, maneuvering through the rocks, climbing the cliff at the shore). Assign at least one playleader to lead each group in constructing their part of the course.

❹ *Before You Begin:* Provide each of the groups with ample materials to create their part of the course. A worktable should be provided for each small group to organize supplies: paint, paintbrushes, etc.

Step-by-Step:

❶ Gather each group in its designated area and introduce the activity.

"We need to build an escape course that will take us from our sinking ship, through the treacherous waters, to the safety of the island. Our group is responsible for building the part of the escape course through this area."

❷ Ask the children to think about what they need to do to escape from the ship to the island and what sort of obstacles might be in their way. As the children generate ideas, ask how they might recreate those things using the materials available.

Example:

Leader: *"What should be the first thing we do when escaping from our sinking ship?"*

Children: *"Jump in the water!"*

Leader: *"How can we pretend we're jumping in the water using these materials?"*

Children might suggest jumping from the balance beam onto the tumbling mat (the balance beam should be low to the ground) while being sprayed by a hose. Or they may suggest painting a sheet or a piece of cardboard blue, which they can then roll across or lay on and pretend they're swimming.

❸ Each group has 90 minutes to plan and create their course section. Once the children have decided how their part of the course will be set up, they can build it with the playleaders' assistance. Make sure the course is safe and that all of the crewmembers will be able to complete it. Encourage the children to think how they might involve everyone in each activity.

Possible Course Activities

- A field of shark fins (made from painted cardboard) that the children must crawl through or walk through blindfolded, guided verbally by another child.

- An underwater cave made from large cardboard boxes or drums with blue sheets over them. Strings can be hung inside the box as seaweed.

- An alligator pit made from a balance beam with painted cardboard alligators placed beneath it.

The possibilities are endless. Be creative!

Activity 3:   The Escape

Time Required: *60 minutes*

Type of Activity: *Culmination; Large Group*

Concept:
Children experience the escape course.

Supplies:
- The escape course created in Activity 2

Preparational Activities:

1 *Prior to Unit Two:* Assign playleaders to conduct children through each section of the course.

2 *Before You Begin:* Make sure that the course is ready to be used: no sharp corners or pointed objects, all objects to be climbed over or under securely fastened if necessary, paint dried, etc.

Step-by-Step:

1 Each group should first go through the section of the course it created. Encourage children to help each other through the course.

2 Once all the groups have gone through their part of the course, they should rotate to the next section and go through it.

3 Continue rotating until each group has experienced all sections of the course.

4 Children can continue playing in the course until it is time to end the workshop and clean up. Gather everyone together in a large group and recap the unit's activities as well as what to look forward to in Unit Three.

ORIENTATION ► ◄ THE EXPERIENCE ► ◄ CULMINATION ►

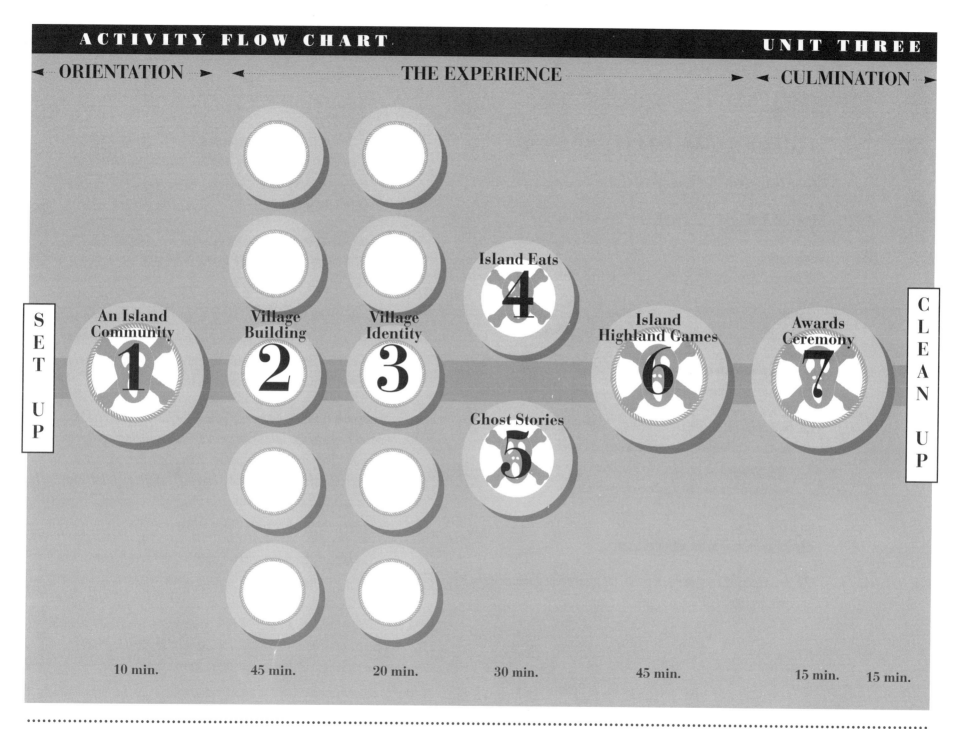

SET UP

CLEAN UP

An Island
Community
1

Village
Building
2

Village
Identity
3

Island Eats
4

Ghost Stories
5

Island
Highland Games
6

Awards
Ceremony
7

10 min.   45 min.   20 min.   30 min.   45 min.   15 min.   15 min.

Activity 1:   An Island Community

Time Required: *10 minutes*

Type of Activity: *Orientation; Large Group*

Concept:
Playleaders orient children to the activities in Unit Three.

Supplies:
- Materials to decorate the meeting space: signs, streamers, etc.

Preparational Activities:

❶ *Prior to Unit Three:* Assign one playleader to conduct the activity.

❷ *Before You Begin:* Decorate the large group meeting area according to the day's theme of arriving on the island and building an island community (e.g., signs saying "Welcome to the Island," "Aloha!" or "If you lived here, you'd be home by now").

Step-by-Step:

❶ Gather children in the large meeting area.

❷ When everyone is gathered together, the playleader sets the stage for the day's activities.

"Congratulations, everyone! We made it to the island. And guess what! It's the island that's shown on our treasure map! Getting here was more difficult than we thought it would be, but we've finally arrived and didn't lose anyone in the storm!

"But our search for buried treasure isn't over yet. This island is large and full of danger. We have to be careful, or the ghost of Long John Silver will spoil our adventure yet.

"If we set off across the island now, we'll surely lose our way and die of hunger. We need to devise a system of survival—a support system that will give us a base from which we can continue our search for the buried treasure.

"We should follow the example of people around the world who have needed the same sort of support system. They've worked together to create the things they need to survive. They've grown food, built shelters, and developed rules about how they can live together. Each person has contributed their skills and talents. They've created communities by working together and depending on each other.

"So we're going to need everyone to help out and work to build our own community here on this island. Without a means of survival, we'll never be able to find the buried treasure. We'll use the wreckage of the ship and other materials we can find here on the island to build our shelters. Remember, we're all in this together and we're all going to have to depend on each other if we're going to survive here."

Activity 2: Village Building

Time Required: *45 minutes*

Type of Activity: *The Experience; Small Groups*

Concept:
Children construct an island settlement.

Supplies:
- PVC Pipe Building System (see "Props and Patterns," page 97)

- Sheets

- Dye in assorted colors

- Dye buckets

- Tempera paints in assorted colors

- Paint containers

- Paintbrushes: large and medium

- String

- Scissors (adult)

- Matt knives

- Cardboard boxes for signs and housebuilding material

- Materials from wrecked ship

- Large worktable(s)

- Decorations for the small group areas

Preparational Activities:

❶ *Prior to Unit Three:* Assign playleaders to each site and decide what part of the village each will build with their crews: housing, mess tent, storehouse, group meeting hall, etc.

❷ Designate sites for the construction of the village. They should be relatively flat and clear.

❸ *Before You Begin:* Divide the materials equally among the sites. The painting supplies should be arranged on a central worktable at each site. The dye should be prepared ahead of time and located near the worktable.

❹ Each leader should carry a matt knife, scissors, string, and tape during the activity. A utility apron is useful for carrying these supplies (see "Playleader Activity Belt," page 96). Children should never use matt knives.

❺ Decorate the small group areas.

Step-by-Step:

1 Divide the children into small groups. These can be the same as the crews from Unit One or the small groups from Unit Two, but they don't have to be.

2 Take each small group to the area where it will be building.

3 Show the children the materials and demonstrate how they work (especially how to connect the PVC pipe and fittings).

4 The children then build their village, working in small groups of 2 to 3 children. The PVC pipe provides the frames for the structures. It can be assembled to form cubes or tent-like triangles.

5 After the frame is completed, sheets can be ripped to size and attached to the frame to form ceilings and walls.

6 If the children want to dye their sheets, this should be done before attaching them to the frame. The sheets can be knotted in many places and dipped in a number of colors for a tie-dye effect.

7 To attach a sheet, rip a diagonal tear about 6 to 8 inches long at the corner of the sheet and tie around the frame. Repeat for all four corners.

8 Sheets can then be painted with tempera paints. Leaders can also assist children in cutting windows and doors.

9 Cardboard can also serve as ceilings and walls. It should be cut to size by the leader with a matt knife. Punch a small hole in each of the four corners and tie the cardboard to the frame with strong string. The cardboard can also be painted with tempera paint.

10 Children can identify their structures using a cardboard sign with their names or a design painted on it. The signs can be hung above the doorway using string.

Activity 3: Village Identity

Time Required: *20 minutes*

Type of Activity: *The Experience; Small Groups*

Concept:
Children develop symbols for their community and create patches and flags.

Supplies:
- Pillowcases

- Scissors

- Safety pins

- Tempera paints in assorted colors, and paint containers

- Paintbrushes: large, medium, and small

- 36-inch bamboo garden stakes

- 6-inch pieces of string

- Large pieces of newsprint

- Large pieces of cardboard

- Marking pens (water-based, assorted colors)

- Masking tape

Preparational Activities:

1 *Before You Begin:* Divide the materials equally among the villages and arrange them on the worktables.

Step-by-Step:

1 The villagers gather to develop their village symbol and decide how they will display that symbol given the materials provided.

2 Mount the newsprint on cardboard and facilitate a group decision making process to develop the village symbol. Children brainstorm ideas as one of the playleaders records them on the large piece of paper. The children can then decide which symbol or combination of symbols they would like to use to represent their village.

3 Once the children have decided on a symbol, they must also decide whether they would like to use the materials they have to create a giant village flag, patches for each village member, or some combination of the two.

4 When the children have decided how they would like to display their village symbol, they use the materials (pillowcases, scissors, and paint) to create the flag and/or patches. Safety pins may be used to attach the pillowcases together and make a large flag or to attach patches to the children's clothing. Use string to tie the flag to the stick.

Activity 4: Island Eats

Time Required: 30 minutes (conducted simultaneously with Activity 5)

Type of Activity: The Experience; PLAE Station (1 of 2)

Concept:
Children prepare food in their village.

Supplies:
- Small paper bowls

- Worktables

- Cardboard for instructional signs

- Measuring spoons: tablespoons, 1/2 teaspoons

- Forks

- Paper plates

- Small containers (e.g., clean cottage cheese cartons to distribute ingredients to substations, if needed)

- Peanut butter (4 tablespoons per child)

- Instant nonfat dry milk (2 tablespoons per child)

- Raisins (2 tablespoons per child)

- Honey (1/2 teaspoon per child)

- Coconut (about 1 tablespoon per child)

NOTE: When calculating how much of each ingredient you will need, keep in mind the following measure equivalents:
- 8 ounces equals 1 cup
- 1 cup equals 16 tablespoons
- 1 tablespoon equals 3 teaspoons

Therefore, a 32-ounce jar of peanut butter will yield 4 cups of peanut butter, which is equal to 64 tablespoons, enough for 16 children to complete the following recipe.

Preparational Activities:

❶ Prior to Unit Three: The activity is organized into a single PLAE Station with as many substations as needed, based on the size of the group. Assign two leaders to work at each substation.

❷ Make cardboard instructional signs for each of the four cooking steps (see "Step-by-Step" below). The signs should be illustrated with drawings to allow children who cannot read to follow the instructions.

❸ Before You Begin: Arrange the work tables at the PLAE Station locations and distribute supplies as follows:

Step One

- Instructional sign
- Paper bowls
- Peanut butter
- Honey
- Tablespoon
- 1/2 teaspoon
- Fork

Step Two

- Instructional sign
- Instant nonfat dry milk
- Tablespoon
- Fork

Step Three

- Instructional sign
- Raisins
- Tablespoon

Step Four

- Instructional sign
- Coconut (put a small amount at a time on a paper plate)
- Paper plate

Step-by-Step:

❶ Children work in small groups.

❷ As they arrive at the substation, playleaders explain the recipe instructions.

❸ Children proceed down the line, performing each step of the activity as they go. Assist as necessary.

4 Following are the cooking instructions that should appear on signs:

Step One: Blend

- Take a paper bowl.
- Measure 4 tablespoons peanut butter into the bowl.
- Measure 1/2 teaspoon honey into the bowl.
- Blend with fork.

Step Two: Add Dry Milk

- Add 2 tablespoons instant nonfat dry milk powder to the mixture.
- Blend with fork.

Step Three: Knead in Raisins

- Add 2 tablespoons raisins to the peanut butter mixture.
- Blend with hands.

Step Four: Roll in Coconut

- Roll peanut butter mixture into small balls with hands.
- Roll balls in coconut.

5 Enjoy! (Makes about 4 balls per child.)

Put 4 tablespoons peanut butter and 1/2 teaspoon honey in a bowl and blend.

Add 2 tablespoons dry milk powder and blend with a fork.

Knead in 2 tablespoons of raisins.

Roll into small balls and cover in coconut.

Activity 5: Ghost Stories

Time Required: *30 minutes (conducted simultaneously with Activity 4)*

Type of Activity: *The Experience; PLAE Station (1 of 2)*

Concept:
Playleaders and children gather in the village to share ghost stories with each other.

Supplies:
• Imagination!

Preparational Activities:

❶ *Prior to Unit Three:* One or more of the playleaders should have a ghost story prepared to share with the children. It can be one that's been told a million times before or a new creation. Make it fun and imaginative, but don't make it more than 5 minutes long (the children will want to tell stories too!).

❷ *Before You Begin:* Locate a spot where the villagers can gather in a large circle to share stories.

Step-by-Step:

❶ Gather the children in a large circle.

❷ The playleader who has prepared a story shares that story with the children.

❸ When the first story is finished, ask the children if they have ghost stories they would like to share with the group. Have the children raise their hands and call on them one at a time.

❹ Encourage the children to keep their stories brief so that as many people as possible can share a story.

Activity 6: Island Highland Games

Time Required: *45 minutes*

Type of Activity: *The Experience; Large Group*

Concept:
Children enjoy a series of games which celebrate their community.

Supplies:
- The games in this section have been selected because they promote community spirit and do not require special equipment. Any game can be adapted to a pirate theme and used during this session. The games included here were adapted from *The New Games Book* (New York: Dolphin Books, 1976) and *More New Games* (New York: Dolphin Books, 1981). If competitive games are used, emphasize "personal best" over competing with others and participating rather than winning.

- Decorations for the game area

- Imagination and enthusiasm!

Preparational Activities:
1 *Prior to Unit Three:* Locate a space that will provide a large, flat playing surface, clear of obstacles. "Octopus" requires two goal lines or base areas that can be easily identified.

2 Assign playleaders to each game; referees should be assigned as needed.

3 *Before You Begin:* Decorate the game area using the flags created in Activity 3 and other materials.

Step-by-Step:
1 Welcome everyone to the Island Highland Games—an event to bring the new villagers together for fun and good times. Introduce the first game and let the fun begin!

2 Following are five games that might be used for your Island Highland Games:

The Island Is It

This game has been called the world's fastest game. The two rules are 1) everybody on the island is "It" and 2) when a player is tagged, he or she is frozen.

The game begins by everybody shouting "What's the name of this game?" The answer is shouted in return and the game starts—and quickly ends.

Pirate Sword

Another variation on the old favorite "Tag," this game has one person who is the Pirate (who is "It"). The Pirate's hands become swords. When a sword touches another child (gently—not with a chopping motion; be sure the Pirates are aware of this), the child who has been tagged must keep one hand on the spot where he or she was wounded by the sword. When tagged again, the twice-wounded villager puts his or her other hand on the second spot. On the third tag, the child is frozen.

Octopus

This game requires two goal lines or base areas at opposite ends of a large area. One child is "the octopus." Everybody else is a fish.

The fish gather at one of the goal or base areas. The octopus stands in the middle of the ocean (the playing field) and calls out, "Fish, fish, swim in my ocean!" The fish oblige by swimming (running, walking, hopping —whatever is agreed upon) across the ocean to the other goal or base. Fish who are tagged freeze and become the octopus's "tentacles."

The fish can now be tagged by either the octopus or one of his tentacles. As more and more fish are tagged, the ocean fills with the octopus's tentacles and the fish have a more and more difficult time crossing. (A twist on the game is to have the frozen players shut their eyes, giving the fish more of a fighting chance.)

Pirate Naming Ceremony

In this game, children create a "conveyer belt" that transforms ordinary children into genuine pirates. It begins with all the players removing any watches and jewelry on their wrists or hands. The group forms two lines facing each other. In each line, the players stand shoulder-to-shoulder with elbows bent, forearms in front, palms up.

Forearms should alternate so that each player's forearm is flanked by the forearms of the players facing him or her. Everyone must bunch together closely, with one foot forward and one foot back for balance. Playleaders should be spaced evenly throughout both lines to help stabilize the pirate "conveyor belt."

Players then take turns, one at a time, becoming pirates. They stand at one end of the conveyer belt (with glasses, belts, etc. off) and announce what they want their pirate name to be. The player then slides onto the conveyer belt and is bounced down to the other end as the other children chant the pirate's chosen name. A playleader is stationed at the far end to help the pirate off the belt (pirates are easily bruised) and the now-pirate joins the conveyer belt.

Long John's Ghost

This game begins with one child designated as Long John's Ghost. The other children remain normal, everyday island citizens, mingling about the playing field as always, except for one difference—everyone's eyes are shut (but not the ghost's!). Designate some playleaders as referees to keep all the players within the boundaries of the game area.

The ghost then does what ghost pirates are known to do—sneak up on unsuspecting island citizens and pounce on them (which in pirate lingo means to grab them, not jump on top of them!), making the sounds that pouncing ghost pirates are wont to make.

Pounced-on island citizens become ghost pirates too. All the ghost pirates rove around, continuing to pounce on the remaining unsuspecting island citizens. The game continues until everyone has become a ghost pirate.

Because this game can be frightening (no one likes being attacked by ghost pirates, especially with closed eyes), children should be made aware that they can choose to join the ghost pirates in their pouncing at anytime.

Activity 7: Awards Ceremony

Time Required: *15 minutes*

Type of Activity: *Culmination; Large Group*

Concept:
All children are recognized for their outstanding achievements.

Supplies:
- Award certificates (one per child)

- Decorations for the large group meeting area

Preparational Activities:

1 *Prior to Unit Three:* Assign at least one playleader to conduct the activity.

2 Photocopy an awards certificate for each child (see "Props and Patterns," page 89) and fill in the child's name.

3 *Before You Begin:* Decorate the large group meeting area.

Step-by-Step:

1 Gather children in the large group meeting area.

2 Review the day's activities and congratulate everyone for a job well-done, calling children forward individually to receive their award.

3 When everyone has received their award, end the unit with a group "Hoorah!" and then ask everyone to join in cleaning up.

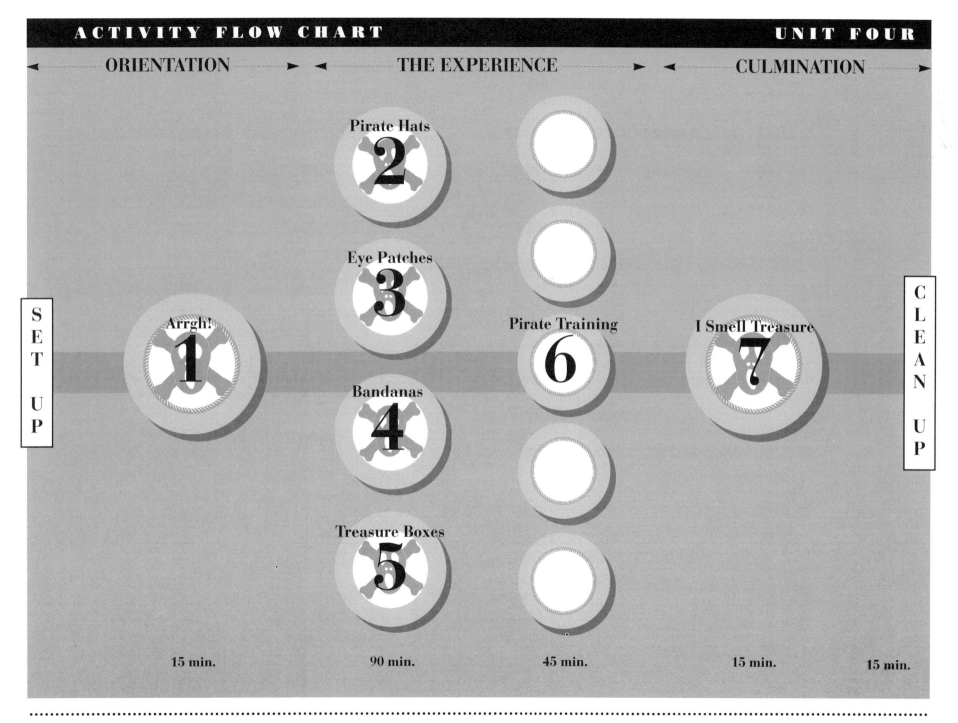

ORIENTATION   THE EXPERIENCE   CULMINATION

SET UP

CLEAN UP

Arrgh!
1

Pirate Hats
2

Eye Patches
3

Bandanas
4

Treasure Boxes
5

Pirate Training
6

I Smell Treasure
7

15 min.   90 min.   45 min.   15 min.   15 min.

Activity 1:   **Arrgh!**

Time Required: *15 minutes*

Type of Activity: *Orientation; Large Group*

Concept:
Playleaders conduct a large group meeting to orient children to the unit's events.

Supplies:
- Decorations for the large group meeting area

- Pirate costume for an adult

Preparational Activities:
❶ *Prior to Unit Four:* Assign a playleader to lead the orientation meeting and present the unit's themes and activities.

❷ *Before You Begin:* Decorate the meeting area with themes for the Unit Four activities (i.e., pirates, preparing for the treasure hunt, etc.).

Step-by-Step:
❶ As children arrive for the unit, assemble them in a large group.

❷ When everyone has arrived, give the orientation talk (in "piratese" to help set the stage).

"Ahoy, blimey limeys! So ye thinks yer goin' ta find the buried treasure of me old friend Long John Silver, do ye? Well, ye should thinks again! Many a brave soul has weathered the same trail, but not a-one has yet found the riches and treasures that were buried so many years ago!

"But I tells ye what. I'll give ye a hand in yer adventure if ye'll promise me a part of the treasure, say a doubloon or two. If an' whenst ye find it.

"Now the problem with the landlubbers who tried ta find the treasure before ye, was that they weren't larned in the ways of pirates. They were easily befuddled by the bands of rovin' pirates who make their home here on the isle o' treasure. If ye wants to be successful an' find the treasure, ye needs ta know how ta thinks an' act like a pirate. An' there ain't nobody better ta teach ye than meself an' me maties here.

*"The first thing ye needs ta do is make yerselves look like pirates. So yer goin' ta have ta put a scowl on yer face and look as mean an' ugly as ye can be. Yer also goin' ta be needin' a patch fer yer eye (we pirates always have a bad eye), a hat fer yer head, an' a bandana fer ta tie around yer forehead and keep the sea salt off yer brow. Of course, ye'll be
needin' a treasure box fer puttin' yer treasure in oncst ye find it, too.*

"So get yer scowls ascowlin', landlubbers, an' make yerselves inta pirates. There's room aplenty at all the different pirate stations, so spread yerselves about an' make yerselves into respectable pirates before the ghost of Long John Silver hears tale of our plan an' pulls another one of his tricks on us!"

Activity 2:   Pirate Hats

Time Required: *90 minutes (conducted simultaneosly with Activities 3, 4, and 5)*

Type of Activity: *The Experience; PLAE Station (1 of 4)*

Concept:
Children construct pirate hats for their pirate costumes.

Supplies:
- White poster board

- Black poster board

- Scissors

- Pencils

- Staplers and staples

- Black fine-point, water-based marking pens

- Hat pattern

- Large worktable(s)

- Masking tape

- Decorations for the PLAE Station

Preparational Activities:

1 *Prior to Unit Four:* Assign playleaders to conduct the activity.

2 Cut out parts to construct pirate hats for all the participants. That will require hat fronts (in black), and hat backs (also in black, see "Props and Patterns," page 95). Each sheet of black poster board should be enough for two hats (backs and fronts).

3 *Before You Begin:* Arrange supplies on the worktables.

4 Decorate the PLAE Station.

Step-by-Step:

❶ Give each child a hat front, a hat back, and materials to decorate the hat as they choose. The white poster board can be used to cut out a "skull and crossbones" or other figure for the front of the hat.

❷ Children can staple their hat fronts and backs together so that their hats fit snugly on their heads. Assist as necessary.

❸ Children can identify their hats by writing their name on a piece of masking tape they affix inside.

❹ When children have completed their hat, they can go to one of the other PLAE Stations that are being operated simultaneously.

Cut out hat fronts and backs from black poster board.

Decorate the hat front using the white poster board and other materials.

Staple the hat front and back together so that it fits snugly on the child's head.

Activity 3:   Eye Patches

Time Required: *90 minutes (conducted simultaneously with Activities 2, 4, and 5)*

Type of Activity: *The Experience; PLAE Station (1 of 4)*

Concept:
Children construct eye patches for their pirate costumes.

Supplies:
- Black vinyl
- Scissors
- Elastic thread
- Large worktable(s)

Preparational Activities:
1 *Prior to Unit Four:* Assign playleaders to conduct the activity.

2 *Before You Begin:* Organize supplies and decorate the PLAE Station.

Step-by-Step:
1 Children use scissors to cut an oval from the black vinyl.

2 They then cut a piece of elastic thread long enough to stretch around their head comfortably—12 inches should be plenty.

3 Using scissors or a hole punch, cut a hole in each side of the oval.

4 The child then puts each end of the thread through a hole and ties it.

5 When the child has finished making an eye patch, he or she can put it on and proceed to one of the other PLAE Stations.

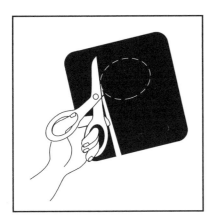

Cut the eye patch shape out of black vinyl.

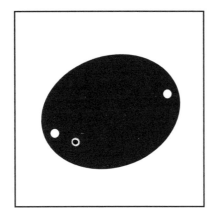

Cut a hole in each side of eye patch.

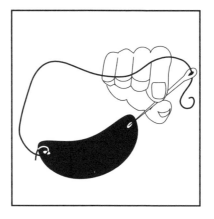

Attach elastic thread, long enough to stretch around the child's head (and still be snug).

Activity 4: Bandanas

Time Required: *90 minutes (conducted simultaneously with Activities 2, 3, and 5)*

Type of Activity: *The Experience; PLAE Station (1 of 4)*

Concept:
Children create bandanas for their pirate costumes.

Supplies:
- Sheets or pillow cases for a 12-inch-square bandana for every child

- Scissors

- Rubberbands

- Fabric dye in assorted colors

- Dye buckets

- Clothesline

- Clothespins or safety pins

- Masking tape

- Ink pens

- Large worktable(s)

- Decorations for the PLAE Station

Preparational Activities:

❶ *Prior to Unit Four:* Assign playleaders to conduct the activity.

❷ Cut squares of cloth from the sheets or pillowcases, large enough to be tied around children's heads or necks as bandanas (approximately 12 inches by 12 inches).

❸ *Before You Begin:* Assemble supplies on the worktable(s).

❹ Hang the clothesline at a height easily reached by the children.

❺ Mix the assorted dyes in the dye buckets and locate them near the PLAE Station.

❻ Decorate the PLAE Station.

Step-by-Step:

❶ Give each child a square of cloth when they arrive at the station.

❷ Children can then tie-dye their bandana by pulling up small sections of the cloth and putting several rubberbands around each clump. Sections of the bandana can then be dipped in several colors of dye. Encourage children to be creative in how they choose to dye their bandana.

❸ When the bandana is dried, have the child remove the rubberbands and hang it on the clothesline with a clothespin or safety pin.

❹ Write the child's name on a small piece of masking tape and attach it to the clothespin or bandana.

❺ As bandanas are drying, children can go to one of the other PLAE Stations that are being operated simultaneously.

❻ When a bandana is completely dried, playleaders can help tie it around the little pirate's head. Children can also help each other do this.

Activity 5:   Treasure Boxes

Time Required: *90 minutes (conducted simultaneously with Activities 2, 3, and 4)*

Type of Activity: *The Experience; PLAE Station (1 of 4)*

Concept:
Children create a box in which to put their treasure.

Supplies:
- Shoeboxes (one per child)

- Duct tape

- Fabric to cover boxes

- Scissors

- White glue

- Glue containers: 16-oz. plastic containers, pint milk cartons, cottage cheese containers, etc.

- Glue brushes

- Decorations for treasure boxes: buttons, stickers, glitter, etc.

- Large worktable(s)

- Decorations for the PLAE Station

Preparational Activities:

1 *Prior to Unit Four:* Assign playleaders to conduct the activity.

2 Tape one side of each shoebox lid to its box with duct tape so that the lid opens like a treasure box or trunk lid.

3 *Before You Begin:* Assemble supplies on the work tables at the PLAE Station.

4 Decorate the PLAE Station.

Step-by-Step:

1 Give each child a shoebox with a taped lid when they arrive at the PLAE Station.

2 Cut a piece of fabric that is large enough to wrap all the way around the box (from the front lip of the open trunk around and over the lid), with approximately one inch extra to wrap over the edges. Two end pieces (large enough to cover each end of the box) should also be cut. Children can cut their own pieces or a playleader can assist them.

3 When the pieces are cut, children can glue them to the box. Decorations can also be added, using the glue and materials provided.

4 When the treasure box is finished, the pirate should write his or her name inside it with a marking pen and move on to one of the other PLAE Stations that are being operated simultaneously.

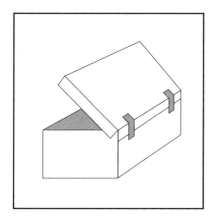

Tape one side of the box lid to the box to create a hinge.

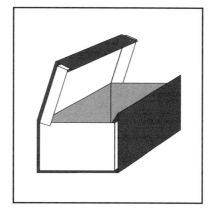

Wrap the box in fabric from the front lip of the open box around and over the lid (attach with glue).

Cover the sides of the box in fabric too.

Decorate in a suitable treasure box theme.

Activity 6:   Pirate Training

Time Required: *45 minutes*

Type of Activity: *The Experience; Small Groups*

Concept:

Children develop their teamwork skills in preparation for the upcoming treasure hunt.

Supplies:

- Strong rope, in approximately 25-foot lengths (two lengths per group)

- Strong string (one roll per group)

- 6-foot poles (two per group) or two trees spaced approximately 10 feet apart

Preparational Activities:

❶ *Prior to Unit Four:* Assign at least one playleader to each small group.

❷ Identify a suitable area for each small group. You will need two poles or trees at least 10 feet apart with clear space in between. The poles must be such that two ropes can be tied between them, one approximately 2 feet off the ground and one approximately 5 feet off the ground.

❸ *Before You Begin:* Tie the ropes to the poles as described in item 2 above. Then tie the string between the two ropes to create "triangles" of different sizes, large enough for the children to pass through (as shown below).

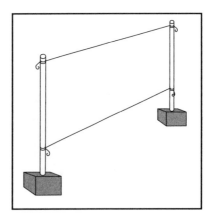

Place the poles about 10 feet apart and tie two ropes between them, one at 2 feet and one at 5 feet.

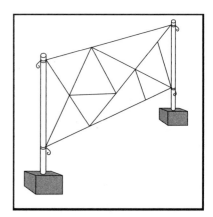

Tie string between the ropes to create triangles of different sizes.

Step-by-Step:

❶ Divide pirates (in costume) into small groups and gather each group at the appropriate small group area. The ideal size of a group for this exercise is between five and eight children.

❷ Introduce the pirates to the activity:

"Now that ye look like pirates, it's time ye larned how ta act like 'em. Yer probably thinkin' that a pirate is mean 'n' dirty, an' real greedy too. But that's because ye don't know nothin' when it comes to piratin'. The mean an' greedy pirates are the ones that git all the attention, cause thar up ta no good. Me mates an' me are different. We may be a bit dirty under the nails, but we know that bein' mean an' greedy won't find us the treasure. If we're goin' ta track it down, we gots ta work like a team.

"Now this here contraption is what I call the pirate's provin' ground. It separates the real pirates from the landlubbers.

"If yer goin' ta make it in the pirate's provin' ground, yer goin' ta have ta work together, an' larn to trust each other. Cuz what yer goin' ta have ta do is help each other git through these openin's in the pirate's net without touchin' the net at all. Nayre a soul I know can do it without help from the pirate crew, cuz we're goin' ta have ta lift ye up and halp balance ye if ye're goin' ta do it right. Ye thinks its an easy thing, but I warn ye, it's enough ta make a landlubber of ye."

❸ Have children take turns trying to maneuver through the triangular openings without touching the string. Other children should help out by boosting, balancing, lifting, or talking to the person who is trying to get through. Everyone has to work together!

❹ Encourage children to try different openings. Can the team get everyone through at least one opening successfully?

Activity 7: I Smell Treasure!

Time Required: *15 minutes*

Type of Activity: *Culmination; Large Group*

Concept:
Playleaders introduce children to the upcoming treasure hunt activities.

Supplies:
- Decorations for the large group meeting area

Preparational Activities:

1 *Prior to Unit Four:* Designate a large group meeting area.

2 Assign one playleader to introduce the Treasure Hunt.

3 *Before You Begin:* Decorate the large group meeting area.

Step-by-Step:

1 Gather all the children in a large group.

2 Recount the unit's activities and introduce the Treasure Hunt:

"It looks as though we're almost ready to begin the Treasure Hunt! Not only do we have the map of where the treasure is buried, but we've made it to the island and eluded the ghost of Long John Silver. We've built an island community, and we've become pirates trained in the ways of pirateering! Looks like we're ready to go!

"When we get together again, we'll be starting our search for Long John Silver's buried treasure.

"Be sure you have all of your equipment: your eye patch, hat, and bandana so that you look like a real pirate, and your treasure box so that you have somewhere to put all the riches we're bound to find! And don't forget what you learned in pirate training—it may come in handy.

"When you come back here for the Treasure Hunt, we'll have maps, compasses, code books, and clues ready for you—everything you'll need to become the richest pirates ever!"

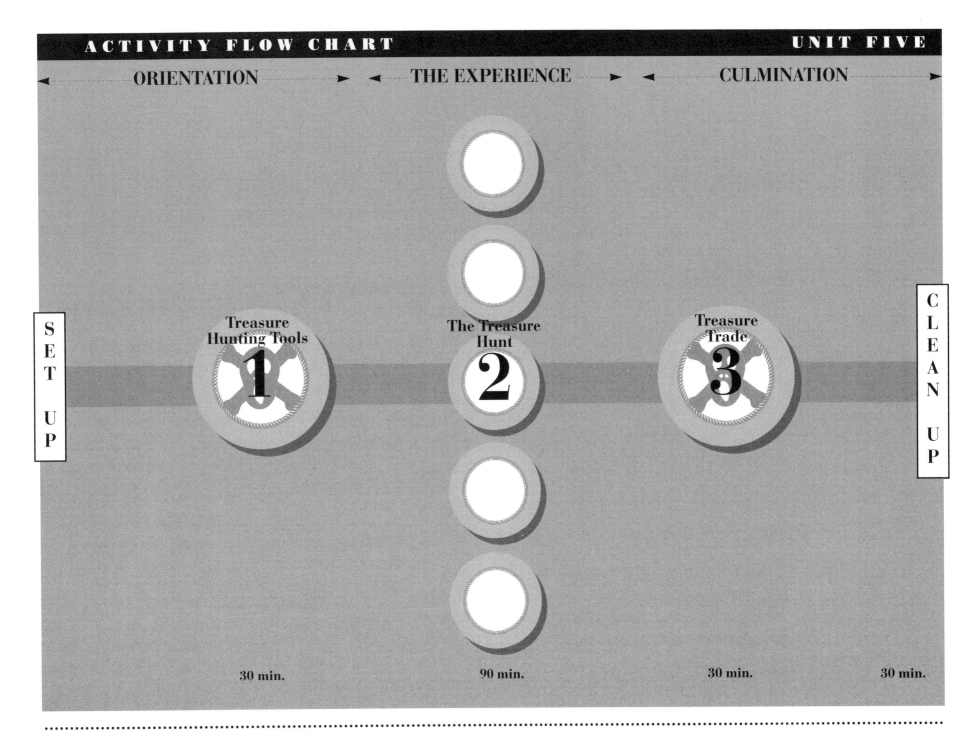

ORIENTATION   THE EXPERIENCE   CULMINATION

SET UP

CLEAN UP

Treasure Hunting Tools
1

The Treasure Hunt
2

Treasure Trade
3

30 min.   90 min.   30 min.   30 min.

Activity 1:   Treasure Hunting Tools

Time Required: *30 minutes*

Type of Activity: *Orientation; Large Group*

Concept:
Children are prepared for the Treasure Hunt and divided into Treasure Hunting Teams.

Supplies:
- String

- Masking tape

- Bottles

- Colored paper (a different color for each team)

- Pens

- Scissors

- Compasses

- Site maps

- Code books (see "Props and Patterns," page 91)

- Treasure chests

- Treasure! (costume jewelry, etc.)

- Treasure boxes (made by children in the previous unit)

- Pirate costumes (made by children in the previous unit)

- Decorations for the large group meeting area

Preparational Activities:
❶ *Prior to Unit Five:* Assign one playleader to introduce the Treasure Hunt.

❷ Assign one playleader to be in charge of each Treasure Hunting Team. Assign a color to each team. As the team searches for the treasure, it should follow only those clues that are the same color.

❸ The Treasure Hunt is the culminating event for the *Treasure Quest* PLAE Score. It requires a fair amount of thought, creativity, and preparation on the part of playleaders to be done well. It is an excellent opportunity to incorporate other curriculum subjects in the program's activities.

The Treasure Hunt consists of a series of clues that a Treasure Hunting Team follows around the program area, ultimately arriving at their treasure chest. Prior to Unit Five, leaders must prepare a site map, a code book, and the clues that each team will follow. Clues should be color-coded by Treasure Hunting Team.

④ Prepare the site map by drawing a simple, easy to read plan of the area in which the treasure hunt will take place. Be sure to include all significant environmental features and landmarks that might help children orient themselves on the map. Clearly demarcate the boundaries of the Treasure Hunt area and be sure that all clues are placed within that area.

⑤ Develop the clues that each team will follow to find the buried treasure. Be creative when developing the clues—the more elaborate the clues are, the more fun the hunt will be. Here are some examples of what types of clues might be included:

Riddle Clues

"I'm tall and green against a sky of blue. Look in my arms and you'll find the next clue."

(The team's next clue is hanging from a tree branch.)

Puzzle Clues

Write the clue on a piece of paper and then cut the paper into ten odd-shaped pieces. Give each child a piece and have the team put it together.

Use-the-Compass Clues

Have the team use their compasses to find their next clue. ("Take 10 paces north and 5 paces east to find the next clue.")

Solve-the-Code Clues

Write the clue in code so that the team can use their code books to decipher the message.

Message-in-a-Bottle Clues

Make the team feel like real pirates when they have to pull the clue sheet out of a bottle!

Site Map Clues

Make the clue an overlay for the children's site maps, marking the overlay with one of the features on the map (so the children know how the overlay should be placed), and placing an "X" where the next clue is or where they'll find their treasure!

Action Clues

Have children complete an action or say a phrase before they find the next clue. Example: "Clap your hands three times. Turn around once and say 'I've seen the ghost of Long John Silver,' then run to the northwest corner of the field to find your next clue."

These are just a few examples. Each team needs enough clues to provide a 90-minute hunt. Be imaginative!

6 Prepare the code book. This will help children decode the clues they find. A general pattern and instructions for a code book are included in "Props and Patterns" on page 91. However, the code book you develop will be customized based on the clues for your Treasure Hunt.

7 Prepare the treasure chests. Treasure chests can be constructed from cardboard or wood and decorated appropriately. Old footlockers, linen chests, or even suitcases can also work well. Remember, finding the treasure chest is the goal of Treasure Quest. An authentic-looking chest adds immeasurably to the fantasy experience.

8 *Before You Begin:* Hide the clues. They should not be easily visible. Set aside the first clue to give to the children at the beginning of the hunt.

9 Divide the treasure equally among the chests and hide the chests in places that will not be obvious to the children as they are conducting their hunts.

10 Divide the treasure hunting materials (site maps, code books, and compasses) equally among the teams.

11 Decorate the program area. Remember—this is the climax!

Step-by-Step:

1 Gather all the children together as a large group to begin the Treasure Hunt. One of the playleaders can begin things when everyone is present:

"Ahoy, maties! Now comes the adventure we've been awaitin' fer. We're ready to set off 'cross the island an' find the buried treasure!

"Now, rumour has it that thar's more than one treasure ta be found. So we're goin' ta divide into Treasure Huntin' Teams an' scour the island. Each Team'll be led by an experienced treasure-huntin' pirate, like meself, but it's goin' ta be up ta you ta figure out the clues and find the treasure. Ta helps ye out, we're goin' ta give each team a map, a code book, an' a compass. Hold onto 'em! Ye'll find they come in handy in yer search for Long John Silver's hidden treasure.

"Each Team'll have different clues they'll be followin' ta find their treasure. Be sure ye only read the clues that are fer yer team. If yer in the blue team, ye only read blue clues. Otherwise, ye'll get lost in the island swamp an' never find yer treasure! An' don't be in too big a hurry. We've plenty a time, an' a rushed hunt always ends in despair."

2 Divide the children into groups with an equal number in each group. The number of Treasure Hunting Teams you have will be based on your group's size, your staffing level, and the size of the area you have for the Treasure Hunt. The ideal size for a Treasure Hunting Team is 5 to 8 children. This allows everyone to participate in solving the clues and finding the treasure.

3 When the teams are divided, playleaders distribute the necessary materials (compass, map, and code book).

Activity 2:   The Treasure Hunt

Time Required: *90 minutes*

Type of Activity: *The Experience; Small Groups*

Concept:
Children hunt for treasure by deciphering and following a series of clues.

Supplies:
• Decorations for clue activity areas (other materials have been provided in Activity 1)

Preparational Activities:
❶ *Before You Begin:* Most of the preparations will have been completed prior to Unit Five. The areas where the Treasure Hunting Teams will find and decipher their clues should be decorated in keeping with the Treasure Hunt theme. Don't let any decorations give away clue locations!

Step-by-Step:
❶ Make sure each team is equipped with all of the necessary equipment (map, code book, compass, treasure boxes).

❷ When everyone is ready, reiterate each team's color. Each team should only read clues of the same color.

❸ Give each team its first clue.

❹ Stay with the teams as they follow their clues and search for their treasure. Make sure teams only read clues that are their color so that they "stay on track."

❺ Congratulate everyone when they find their treasure!

Activity 3:   **Treasure Trade**

Time Required: *30 minutes*

Type of Activity: *Culmination; Large Group*

Concept:
The children trade the treasure.

Supplies:
- Treasure

- Treasure boxes

Preparational Activities:
❶ *Prior to Unit Five:* Be aware of how much treasure is in the treasure chest and how it will be divided equally between the children in each group.

Step-by-Step:
❶ Once children have found their treasure, have them carry it to a central area.

❷ Open the chest!

❸ The playleaders should be responsible for dividing the treasure equally among the children in each group. Since each chest contains the same treasure, each leader should divide the chests equally so that all children receive the same amount and type of treasure.

❹ When the treasure is divided, the children can trade with one another so that everyone winds up with the treasure they like most!

IV. Props and Patterns

A PLAE SCORE RELIES ON IMAGINATION AND INGENUITY, BUT A LITTLE HELP ALONG THE WAY DOESN'T HURT.

On the following pages you will find assistance in the form of prop-making instructions and patterns for use in making your own Treasure Quest.

he "Certificate of Honor" on the back of this page can be photocopied on colored paper and distributed at the Awards Ceremony in Activity 7 of Unit Three. It recognizes the outstanding contributions of all workshop participants.

Certificate of Honor

Hear Ye, Hear Ye.
Let it be known, from this day forth, that

_____

is a person of outstanding valor and commendable courage who,
having been stranded on a strange and dangerous island,
did contribute to the construction of a new community and did celebrate
that community in a spirit of cooperation and friendship.

Deciphering a treasure map can be hard work. Use the signs and symbols on the following pages to provide clues on your treasure map. Then photocopy and assemble a code book for each treasure hunter following the directions below. Use additional pages to present your own customized symbols!

Photocopy code book pages 1 and 2, front to back. Photocopy the cover onto colored cardstock.

Assemble the pages in order.

Staple and fold.

PLAE SCORE™

Treasure Quest

Code Book

Signs & Symbols

 Treasure split up and buried in directions of arrows.

 Danger ahead.

 Treasure is buried in box or chest.

 Beware of pit.

 Go to tall tree in the direction indicated by the treetop.

 Knife points towards treasure.

 Start Here.

 Follow path in direction of arrow.

 Stop at this spot and look for next clue.

 Follow water's edge.

 Note under a rock.

Follow path to the left.

 Follow path in opposite direction of arrow.

 Go back the way you came.

 Seek grove of trees in the direction shown.

 A snake means treasure buried here.

 Follow stream to waterfall.

 Follow path to the right.

 Proceed to center of a circle of rocks or stones.

 Proceed 1/4 of the way around the lake to the left.

 Proceed exactly 1/2 way around the lake to the right.

 Cross over water.

 Mule shoe: keep traveling along path.

Transform those landlubbers into salty dogs with the pirate hat pattern below. Simply enlarge the pattern 160 to 200 percent, cut out two patterns from black poster board, staple them together, and add your favorite "skull 'n' crossbones" or other seafaring design. Refer to the instructions in Activity 2 of Unit Four (pages 71 and 72).

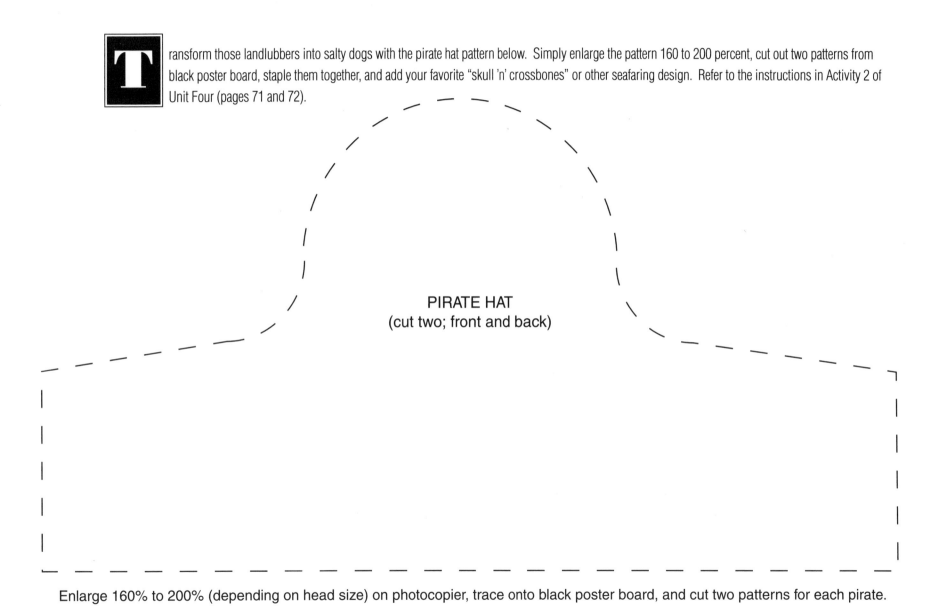

PIRATE HAT
(cut two; front and back)

Enlarge 160% to 200% (depending on head size) on photocopier, trace onto black poster board, and cut two patterns for each pirate.

A simple utility belt can be a great help to playleaders who need quick and convenient access to a host of tools and other implements at a moment's notice. It can also provide a safe place for carrying tools that shouldn't be left lying around (such as scissors or a hammer).

Most hardware stores carry such items and may even be convinced to donate them to your cause. Or you might try checking with a local contractor or construction outfit to see if they have any old utility belts lying around that they wouldn't mind parting with.

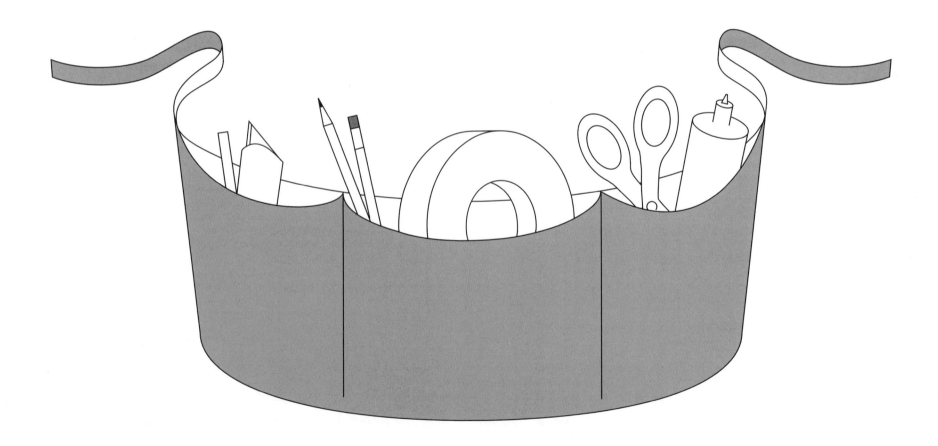

PVC (polyvinyl chloride) pipe is a durable, lightweight material that is invaluable for constructing play props. With a variety of pipe lengths, joint types, and imagination, you can construct nearly anything, from a voting booth to a spaceship.

Once you have your framework built, you can use a number of materials to create walls, ceilings, doors, windows, signs, and decorations. Bedsheets or large pieces of cardboard are a low-cost material that can be tied or taped to your pipe framework and decorated with dyes, paints, and markers.

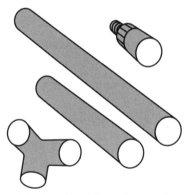

Collect a variety of pipe lengths and different types of joints. The most useful joint is called a "90 degree side-out." You will also need a 3/4" male adapter.

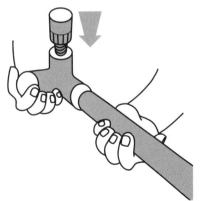

Join the pipes together using the joints. The male adapter is needed to make the 1/2" arm of the joint into a 3/4" arm.

To Get Started:

Find a local source for obtaining PVC pipe. A local hardware store, garden store, or irrigation supply company should have it available or know where you can obtain it. You want PVC pipe that is 3/4-inches in diameter and thick-walled.

To construct one cube, you will need a dozen pipe lengths (5-feet is a good length for a house-size cube), eight "90-degree, side-out" corner joints (these are three-cornered joints with two 3/4" arms and one 1/2" arm), and eight male 1/2" to 3/4" adapters (these are used to make the 1/2" arm of the joint into a 3/4" arm). We recommend pipes in 5-foot lengths (pipes usually come in 10-foot lengths, so all you have to do is cut them in half). However, a variety of lengths and different types of joints are the key to creative structures. Try to collect as many types as possible!

Before allowing children to use the pipes, be sure that all of the cut ends are sanded smooth. For best results, use a cutter specifically designed for PVC pipes.

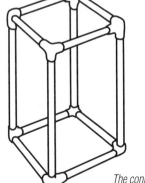

Once you have a kit of parts, store it in a safe place and guard it jealously. It can quickly become your program's most valued asset!

The connected tubes provide the frame for a house, a fort, a spaceship—whatever your imagination desires!

What's a sign-up scroll without an appropriate banner heading? Photocopy the banner graphic onto yellow paper (enlarge it as much as possible), cut it out, and paste it to the top of a large sheet of newsprint. Burn and tear the edges of the newsprint to give it an authentic just-out-of-the-bottle look.

Enlarge onto yellow paper, cut out, and paste on large paper scroll.

NOTES

NOTES